Everything
Tofu

Library and Archives Canada Cataloguing in Publication
Title: Everything tofu : Easy. Delicious. Tofu / Eve-Lyne Auger.
Other titles: Totalement tofu. English
Names: Auger, Eve-Lyne, author.
Description: Translation of: Totalement tofu. | Includes index.
Identifiers: Canadiana 2024045426X | ISBN 9780778807278 (softcover)
Subjects: LCSH: Cooking (Tofu) | LCSH: Tofu. | LCGFT: Cookbooks.
Classification: LCC TX814.5.T63 A9413 2025 | DDC 641.6/5655—dc23

Editor: Marianne Prairie
Translation editor: Amy Treadwell
Proofreader: Kelly Jones
Design: Grace Cheong
Layout and Production: PageWave Graphics Inc.
Cover Photography: Ariel Tarr
Interior Photography: Ariel Tarr
Food Styling: Chantal Legault
Food Styling Assistant: Eve-Lyne Auger
Makeup: Jean-François Casselman-Dupont
Additional photography pages 10, 11, 13 and 14: © Shutterstock

We acknowledge the support of the Government of Canada.
Canada

Published by Robert Rose Inc.
120 Eglinton Avenue East, Suite 800, Toronto, Ontario, Canada M4P 1E2
Tel: (416) 322-6552 Fax: (416) 322-6936
www.robertrose.ca

Printed and bound in China

1 2 3 4 5 6 7 8 9 ESP 33 32 31 30 29 28 27 26 25

Everything Tofu

Easy. Delicious. Tofu.

EVE-LYNE AUGER

Robert
ROSE

From Zero to Hero

I wish I'd had this book around 10 years ago, when I started getting interested in vegetarian food and cooking.

At that time, I thought tofu was only for vegetarians and that I had to eat it if I wanted to adopt that kind of diet. There was just one small problem: I hated tofu. If someone had told me then that one day I would write a book all about tofu, I wouldn't have believed it! In those days, I called it a "beige, boring, rubbery block." As you can see, tofu didn't have a special place in my heart . . .

I clearly remember the first time I ate tofu. I must have been seven years old. My mother had decided to make a special soup: an Asian broth that contained this "new" ingredient. I was puzzled when I saw the small, pale cubes floating on the surface of my bowl of soup. I'd never seen a food like this before. My dad, my sister and I tasted it, and the consensus was "This is terrible!" We still describe it as "kinch soupe."[1] We couldn't swallow more than a mouthful, and it was clear that I never wanted to eat tofu again.

After becoming a vegetarian in 2016, I decided it was time to try tofu again. My second attempt was inconclusive: I lightly fried some thick slices of plain tofu, to which I added a little sesame oil, soy sauce and sesame seeds. Let's just say it didn't have much flavor – just soy and

1 According to the young Daphné Auger (my sister, age 3 at the time), "kinches" were stinky socks. It would be hard to find a better word to give you an idea of the smell and taste of that soup!

sesame – and the texture wasn't that pleasing. A few weeks later, I had the idea to grate a block of tofu with my cheese grater. I then generously sprinkled the grated tofu with hot sauce to use as a filling in a burrito. That was it – I had done it: I now loved tofu!

I had fun in the following months transforming it and cooking it in various ways, using seasonings that gave it a lot of flavor. I was amazed to see how quick it was to prepare and, above all, how versatile it was and how easy to incorporate into many recipes.

Since then, it is always one of the first foods I add to my weekly shopping list. In my online magazine *La Fraîche*, it's also the vegetarian ingredient my readers cook with most, based on the rankings of the most-viewed recipes. However, tofu is still misunderstood by many people who are stuck in the "beige, boring, rubbery block" stage.

If that describes your view of tofu, this book is for you. If you already like tofu, this book is also for you. I hope you will find in these pages everything you need to (re)discover tofu and become aware of its massive culinary potential. I hope my recipes will whet your appetite and will allow you, too, to make tofu a favorite ingredient when it's time to make your shopping list.

Contents

LEGEND FOR GRAPHICS

VEGAN
This icon assures you that a recipe is 100% vegan. However, you can always use vegan products in the vegetarian recipes!

PREPARE THE DAY BEFORE
This icon tells you that part of the recipe needs to be made ahead.

TOOLS
To get the desired result, some recipes require certain tools. These three icons indicate which one to take out of the cupboard.

BLENDER   ELECTRIC MIXER   FOOD PROCESSOR

BASIC RECIPES
This small box tells you where to find the basic recipe you need to make a dish.

Basic Recipe p. ###

The ABCs of Tofu

What Is Tofu?

Tofu, originally from Asia, is a processed food made from soybeans. It is also known as soy cheese because its manufacturing process involves the curdling of soy beverage, a little like curdling milk to make cheese.

To make tofu, we start by soaking dried soybeans. We then crush the beans, boil them and extract the liquid: the soy beverage. This liquid is then coagulated and pressed to make blocks of tofu. The blocks can have different textures, depending on the coagulant used and how long they are pressed. We'll come back to that.

A BRIEF (AND MYSTERIOUS) HISTORY OF TOFU

It is hard to know exactly when tofu was invented, as it is not mentioned in writings before the year 950. According to legend, it was created by accident more than 2,000 years ago. Four different stories have circulated, but none have been proven to be true. The most popular is that someone accidentally dropped coagulant in a soy beverage mixture, causing it to curdle, which led to the creation of tofu. In fact, we can't pinpoint the specific inventor, but we know that the Chinese were the first to make it. Manufacturing was inspired by techniques for coagulating cow's milk, which was then used with soy beverage. Tofu was first adopted by the poorest social classes, around the 10th century, as it cost less than beef but was just as nutritious. Embraced next by Buddhist monks who followed a vegetarian diet, it finally became popular around the 15th century as an essential food in meatless meals for the Chinese Lunar New Year.

SOYBEANS

MAKING TOFU

Over time, tofu manufacturing was perfected and was adopted by other Asian countries, especially Japan and Korea. In each of these regions, tofu became a key element of the local cuisine, with variations in texture and in specific uses.

Tofu became known more widely thanks to world exploration. Europeans encountered it fairly early, around the 16th century, when they tried it during their travels in Asia, often describing tofu as "cheese." However, as it was not universally popular, it wasn't until the 20th century that tofu finally gained ground in the West and started to be adopted by the French, the British and North Americans.

The Asian cuisine craze at the end of the 20th century allowed tofu to take its place on Western plates, even though for a long time it was seen as (and often still is today) a food reserved for vegetarians and vegans.

Why Eat Tofu?

I'll start with the simple answer: because it's good. And at a time when topics like the environmental crisis and inflation are on everyone's lips, I'll add this: because tofu is a local, healthy, affordable and quick-cooking food.

TOFU IS AN ECOLOGICAL LOCAL FOOD

Did you know that Canada and the United States are among the world's largest producers and exporters of legumes? More specifically, "In Canada, Ontario, Quebec and Manitoba are major producers of soybeans, the key ingredient for making tofu; in the United States, Illinois, Iowa and Minnesota are the top soybean-producing states.

Soybeans are grown to meet dietary, economic and environmental needs. Legumes are valued in regenerative agriculture[2] because they have the capacity to improve the health of the soil. Today, many farms are choosing to add soybeans to their crop rotation: they help return atmospheric nitrogen to soil that has been depleted by another crop.

On the consumer side, the demand for vegetarian and vegan dietary solutions has grown by leaps and bounds in recent years. This demand has stimulated local production, making space for more and more tofu manufacturers. Now, tofu has carved out a place in supermarket refrigerators and in people's homes. By buying local tofu, consumers help to reduce the environmental footprint related to transporting food over long distances and promote sustainable agriculture by using local soybean crops.

SOYBEAN FIELD IN BROMONT, QUEBEC

2 A type of agriculture that advocates for an overall approach and aims for not only the regeneration of the soil but also that of other common natural elements, such as the air, water and biodiversity.

TOFU IS HEALTHY AND NUTRITIOUS

In my reading and research over the past 10 years, I learned that soy (and, in turn, tofu) was a food to emphasize as part of a healthy diet, whether you're an omnivore, a vegetarian or a vegan. So, I thought it would be useful to talk about it with my friend Béatrice Dagenais, a dietary technician, to find out more.

TOFU'S NUTRITIONAL PROFILE
By Béatrice Dagenais

To vary the main source of protein in a meal, tofu is really a great option! Soy is a complete protein, which means it contains all the essential amino acids that your body needs.

Firm tofu offers a good daily allowance of iron, magnesium and calcium. Even though the iron in tofu is not absorbed as well by the body as the heme iron found in meat, tofu's iron content is still good. Note that, depending on how the tofu is processed, calcium and magnesium levels can vary from one brand to another. There is also a difference in nutritional values when we compare firm tofu and soft tofu. Firm tofu has a higher nutritional value: because it contains less water, its nutrients are more concentrated.

Another upside of eating tofu: it contains good fats, such as monounsaturated and poly-unsaturated fats, and it is low in saturated fat, which is good news for our heart health!

TOFU IS GOOD FOR YOUR WALLET

Of all the protein choices on the market, tofu is without question an affordable source: $3\frac{1}{2}$ oz (100 g) of tofu costs half as much as $3\frac{1}{2}$ oz (100 g) of meat. At a time when food prices are going up and up, that's a real plus. Also, tofu keeps for a long time when it is properly stored, which means you can buy it in larger quantities without worrying about food waste. Just one more reason to make sure it's always on your shopping list.

TOFU IS THE EPITOME OF SIMPLICITY IN COOKING

Many people say tofu has no taste. They're not totally wrong. But its neutral, mild, delicate flavor is far from being a bad thing. On the contrary, I would say this is its greatest strength! It can be used in almost infinite ways, both savory and sweet, as it takes on the flavor of the ingredients you add.

Also, you can eat it raw or cooked, which reduces stress at mealtimes; with tofu, there are no health risks if a dish is not completely cooked! The result: cooking time is much shorter compared to other foods, allowing you to save lots of time in the kitchen.

AN INCREDIBLY VERSATILE FOOD

Thanks to its neutral taste and varied textures, tofu can blend easily into almost every recipe. It's a real chameleon, taking on and maintaining whatever shape you give it. To help you make the most of its potential, I decided to make you a list of the different ways you can cook it and explore its culinary versatility.

- Eat it raw
- Use it in sauce
- Grind it
- Grate it
- Crumble it (and add it to a mixture)
- Cut it (into every shape imaginable)
- Break it up with your hands
- Pan-fry it
- Roast it
- Bread it and fry it
- Barbecue it
- Stew it

TYPES OF TOFU
1 – SOFT
2 – MEDIUM-FIRM
3 – EXTRA-FIRM
4 – SMOKED

FORMS OF TOFU

5 – GRATED
6 – SLICED
7 – CRUMBLED
8 – CUBED
9 – IN STRIPS
10 – CREAMED

Different Textures of Tofu

At the supermarket, the number of tofu products is constantly increasing, which is wonderful for all of us! You can find it in many shapes, in various types of packaging and with different textures: silken, soft, medium-firm, firm, extra-firm. Depending on the desired result, manufacturers will use a specific coagulant. The pressure placed on the block of coagulated tofu will also be adjusted to achieve the desired firmness – the more water removed, the firmer the block will be.

HOW TO CHOOSE THE RIGHT TOFU

There is tofu for all tastes and for all types of recipes you want to make. However, it's not always easy to find the right texture of tofu simply based on what the package says. For example, if you need extra-firm tofu, one that says "extra-firm" on the package could be a bit too soft for what you want to use it for. I have bought some for crumbling, to get a texture like ground meat, and ended up with something that was a bit softer than I wanted. What do you do when that happens?

First, do your own tests: try different brands to find the one that has the texture you like.

Another tip is to look at the list of ingredients and find the coagulant used in making the tofu:

- Magnesium chloride / calcium chloride: gives a very firm texture (used in the production of extra-firm or medium-firm tofu);
- Calcium sulfate: gives a smoother and more pliable texture (used in the production of firm tofu and silken tofu);
- Glucono-delta-lactone: gives a jellylike texture (used in the production of silken tofu and soft tofu).

You can also simply use the reference chart on the opposite page. I tested the different products available at the supermarket, based on the information on the packaging, to guide you to the best choice for how you want to use it. As I didn't identify the brands, the information in the chart doesn't replace buying and testing different kinds of tofu at home, but the chart could be a useful shortcut.

TEXTURES OF PLAIN TOFU AND THEIR USES

This list shows the types of tofu available in most supermarkets. You will find more varieties in specialty food stores or Asian food stores. They are listed in order from softest to firmest.

TYPE OF PACKAGING / DESCRIPTION	CONSISTENCY	USE
IN A TUB PACKED IN WATER		
Soft tofu	Very soft – very fragile	Raw and cooked, puréed or in sauce or in drinks, stewed
Silken tofu	Soft – can be handled, but with care	Raw and cooked, puréed or in sauce or in drinks, stewed
Medium-firm tofu	Fairly solid and smooth	Raw and cooked, crumbled, boiled
Firm tofu	Solid – very moist – crumbles easily	Raw and cooked, crumbled, boiled, fried, pan fried, grilled
Extra-firm tofu	Very solid – very moist	Raw and cooked, crumbled, boiled, fried, grilled
VACUUM PACKED		
Medium-firm tofu	Solid – spongy – crumbles easily	Raw and cooked, crumbled, boiled
Firm tofu	Fairly solid – dense	Raw and cooked, crumbled, boiled, fried, roasted, sautéed, stewed
Extra-firm tofu	Very solid – very dense	Raw and cooked, crumbled, boiled, fried, roasted, sautéed, stewed

Types of Tofu Used in This Book

When it comes to tofu texture, I have certain preferences: very soft, solid but soft, extremely firm, or dry and smoked. So, I decided to stick to four ways of describing the texture of the tofus you should use in my recipes: soft, medium-firm, extra-firm, and smoked. Each texture is selected specifically to allow you to obtain the same results as I did.

Here is what you will need to make my recipes:

1 **SOFT TOFU** (in a tub). A very soft, fairly fragile tofu with a texture that resembles flan. Once it is crushed, the texture is very smooth and creamy.

2 **MEDIUM-FIRM TOFU** (in a tub or vacuum packed). A block of tofu that keeps its shape, is not too dense; it's fairly spongy and crumbles easily.

3 **EXTRA-FIRM TOFU** (vacuum packed). The brick of tofus. A very solid, very dense, nearly dry tofu.

4 **SMOKED TOFU** (vacuum packed). A very solid, dry-smoked tofu.

Don't worry: you can always use a firm tofu to replace the extra-firm tofu called for in my recipes, but you may not get the exact result expected. It will taste just as good, but the texture might be a bit different!

Tofu Cooking Chart

To encourage you to experiment with tofu, here is a cooking chart based on texture (soft, medium-firm, extra-firm). Please note that cooking times and temperatures may vary based on the size of your tofu pieces. Use these guidelines as a reference and adjust them based on your needs and preferences. On this subject, see "The secret to making tofu that everyone will talk about" on page 22 to discover all my tips for making the texture crispier or more tender, depending on what you prefer.

TOFU COOKING CHART

TYPE OF TOFU	COOKING METHOD	AVERAGE COOKING TIME	TEMPERATURE (IF APPLICABLE)
Soft Tofu	Saucepan (broth, sauce, stew)	15 to 20 minutes	Medium
Medium-firm tofu	Pan (scrambled)	10 to 15 minutes	Medium-high
	Oven (roasted)	20 to 25 minutes	400°F–430°F (200°C–220°C)
	Air fryer	15 to 20 minutes	350°F (180°C)
	Deep fryer	8 to 12 minutes	350°F (180°C)
	Saucepan (broth, soup, stew)	15 to 20 minutes	Medium
Extra-firm tofu	Pan (sautéed)	15 to 20 minutes	Medium-high
	Oven (roasted)	25 to 30 minutes	425°F–450°F (220°C–230°C)
	Barbecue	15 to 20 minutes	Medium-high
	Air fryer	15 to 20 minutes	400°F (200°C)
	Deep fryer	8 to 12 minutes	350°F (180°C)
	Saucepan (broth, soup, stew)	20 to 25 minutes	Medium
	Slow cooker	2 to 3 hours	Low

The Secret to Making Tofu That Everyone Will Talk About

When it's prepared well, tofu is a delight. But I have a secret to share with you: it is possible to make it even better, truly addictive and irresistible. How? Just choose one or more of these tips. They are all accessible, simple to do and make a big difference. Seriously: you will manage to turn someone who may be very reluctant to even try eating tofu into someone who loves it. But if, for some strange reason, the person isn't converted, that means more tasty leftovers for you to enjoy!

You will notice that these tips are not always mentioned in the recipe instructions in this book – but they're always included when they're essential. But know that you can always use one or more at a time if you want to prepare tofu that really stands out.

SEASON IT

This sounds obvious, but too often we neglect to add the proper seasoning. This involves salt and pepper as well as spices: don't be shy about adding a good amount and tasting it to make sure your tofu is brimming with flavor.

BLOT IT / DRAIN IT

Some people do this every time, and others never do, but blotting tofu with a clean cloth or draining it in a colander is a simple trick that lets you dry a medium-firm or extra-firm block of tofu, or remove as much moisture as you can from a block of soft tofu. That way you avoid having too much water in your recipe and the texture stays as stable as possible.

FREEZE IT

Frozen tofu has a slightly different texture than fresh tofu. It becomes more porous and better absorbs marinades and sauces, which can be very useful in some cases. Its texture will also become firmer, so freezing is a good technique to use for stir-frying or frying.

You can freeze it in its original sealed packaging but be sure to cook it as soon as it is thawed to respect its best-before date when you thaw it. I prefer to cut up the tofu before freezing it. This makes it easier to prepare and, because it's frozen in smaller pieces, it will absorb marinades, sauces and seasonings really well after it thaws.

USE CORNSTARCH

Cornstarch brings crispness! Cornstarch and medium-firm or extra-firm tofu should (almost) always work together when you want crispy tofu without using a deep fryer. It dries the surface of the tofu and creates a thin layer that will brown when it comes into contact with a pan and hot fat.

PRECOOK IT

This technique is used to change the texture of medium-firm or extra-firm tofu and to make it look a bit more like meat or to make it crispier. Precook your tofu before adding any seasoning, sauce or marinade, then cook it again. Roast it for a few minutes in the oven, sauté it in a pan or put it in the air fryer before preparing it as directed in your recipe.

CHOOSE THE RIGHT SIZE OF PIECES

The smaller the pieces of tofu, the more flavor it will have. In my view, medium-firm or extra-firm tofu is better when it is broken up properly. I say "broken up" because you will rarely see me cutting a block of tofu into cubes. To give it a look and texture that resembles meat, I use my fingers to break it into (fairly large or tiny) pieces or strips or to crumble it. In addition to giving it a nice texture, this technique allows the tofu to be more flavorful, as seasonings or the marinade stick to the surface better.

MARINATE IT

To make the middle of your pieces of medium-firm and extra-firm tofu extra tasty, take the time to marinate it: the flavors will be heightened. To optimize the effects, make sure to cut up your tofu block or break it up by hand. You can also combine other tips, such as freezing it, blotting it and/or precooking it before placing it in the marinade. To get you started, I have three marinades for you on the next page!

COOK IT IN BUTTER

I got this tip from Jason Charland, owner of the Quebec tofu company Sojà d'ici. This great connoisseur and manufacturer of tofu told me it changed everything. Can you believe I had never tried it? You can use butter made from cow's milk or vegan butter. This brings a nice touch of umami to all your recipes (and is wonderful for cooking smoked tofu!).

Three Marinades for Tastier Tofu

To add more flavor to your medium-firm or extra-firm plain tofu, here are three versatile marinades. They are easy to make, use only a few ingredients and go with almost anything!

Garlic and lemon marinade

INGREDIENTS
3 tbsp (45 mL) olive oil
Juice of 1 lemon
3 garlic cloves, finely chopped
1 tbsp pure maple syrup
1 tbsp chopped fresh parsley (optional)
Salt and pepper
1 lb (454 g) medium-firm or extra-firm tofu, cut as desired

Honey-mustard marinade

INGREDIENTS
2 tbsp (40 g) liquid honey (or pure maple syrup to make it vegan)
2 tbsp (30 g) Dijon mustard
2 tbsp (30 mL) tamari sauce (or soy sauce)
1 tbsp olive oil
1 tbsp lemon juice
1 tsp paprika
1 tbsp chopped fresh chives (optional)
Salt and pepper
1 lb (454 g) medium-firm or extra-firm tofu, cut as desired

Fresh herb marinade

INGREDIENTS
¼ cup (60 mL) olive oil
Zest and juice of 1 lime
2 garlic cloves, finely chopped
¼ cup (60 mL) chopped fresh herbs (such as parsley, basil, chives, cilantro or dill)
Salt and pepper
1 lb (454 g) medium-firm or extra-firm tofu, cut as desired

DIRECTIONS (for the three marinades)

1   In a container that can be sealed, combine all the marinade ingredients except the tofu. Add the pieces of tofu and coat them well with the marinade.

2   Seal the container and let the tofu marinate in the fridge overnight or for up to 24 hours.

3   Once it is marinated, cook the tofu as is (in the oven, frying pan or air fryer) or use it raw in the recipe you've chosen.

1

2

3

4

Making Tofu at Home

Making your own tofu is an amazing experience, especially if you are passionate about cooking. The process may seem complicated and it requires patience, but it has many benefits.

FRESHNESS AND QUALITY OF INGREDIENTS

When you make your own tofu, you have total control over the ingredients. You can choose high-quality soybeans and other fresh ingredients, which can affect the flavor and the texture of the tofu. Also, very few tofu blocks sold in the supermarket have the fresh and delicate taste of tofu made in the traditional way.

PERSONALIZATION

Did you know you can flavor your homemade tofu blocks? My friend Jason Charland, a tofu manufacturer, taught me that. When making various types of tofu, he adds seasonings to his soy beverage mixture so the blocks are flavored all the way through. You can infuse your soy beverage with garlic, fresh herbs, hot pepper flakes or citrus zest, or you can use a spice mixture or even sweeten it. The possibilities are nearly endless, allowing you to obtain a unique and delicious block of tofu.

ECONOMICAL

Making your own tofu can be cheaper than buying it at the store, especially if you eat it regularly. The basic ingredients are usually affordable, and the total cost may be lower than for commercial products.

ECOLOGICAL

Homemade food is always very ecological. By making our own tofu, we avoid plastic packaging and the transport of several products. Also, it's easy to get soybeans in bulk to make it.

STAGES OF MAKING TOFU AT HOME
1 – SOAKING
2 – SOY BEVERAGE
3 – COAGULATION
4 – HOMEMADE TOFU BLOCK

How to Make Firm Tofu

SOAKING	PREPARATION	RESTING	MAKES	KEEPS FOR
8 hours	30 min	35 min	1 block	5 days in the fridge

MATERIALS
Skimmer spoon
Cheesecloth
Tofu press* (optional)
Colander

INGREDIENTS
Homemade soy beverage
2 cups (400 g) plain dried soybeans
8 cups (2 L) water, for soaking
12 cups (3 L) water, divided, for
  processing

DIRECTIONS
Homemade Soy beverage

1 Sort the dried beans, discarding any damaged ones.

2 Place the dried beans in a large dish and cover with the soaking water. Make sure there is at least ¾ inch (2 cm) water over the beans. Soak for at least 8 hours in the fridge.

3 After soaking, drain the beans in a colander and rinse thoroughly.

4 In a blender or food processor, place half the rinsed beans and half the water for processing. Blend for 1 to 2 minutes, or until smooth. Transfer the mixture to a large saucepan. Repeat the process with the remaining half of the beans and remaining water and transfer the mixture to the saucepan.

5 Over high heat, bring the contents of the saucepan to a boil. Reduce the heat to medium-low and simmer for 15 minutes. Remove the foam that forms on the surface periodically with the skimmer spoon. Remove from the heat and let cool.

6 Line a large bowl with cheesecloth. Pour the contents of the saucepan into the lined bowl. Gather the cheesecloth and squeeze well to extract all the liquid (homemade soy beverage) and save the pulp, called okara,** inside the cheesecloth.

7 Use the homemade soy beverage to make tofu or pour it into a sealable container, seal and store for up to 5 days in the fridge.

Tofu

1½ tsp nigari (magnesium chloride), calcium chloride or calcium sulfate*** (gypsum) coagulant

4 tsp water

6 cups (1.5 L) homemade soy beverage

* If you enjoy making your own tofu and want to do it again, you can get a tofu press that allows you to make tofu in a rectangular block like the ones sold in supermarkets (step 12). You can find these in specialty kitchen equipment stores, in natural food stores and online.

** Okara is the soy pulp that builds up in the cheesecloth as the soy beverage is filtered. To avoid food waste, you can add it to your recipes (muffins, smoothies, and others) to increase the protein content and the nutritional value. It keeps for up to 5 days in the fridge in a sealed container.

*** The coagulants listed are available in natural food stores and online.

**** For extra-firm tofu, remember: the heavier the weight and the longer the tofu sits, the firmer the tofu will be. Check the tofu frequently until it reaches the firmness you want.

Tofu

8 In a bowl, dissolve the coagulant in water. Set aside.

9 In a saucepan over medium heat, heat the soy beverage until it simmers.

10 Remove from the heat and pour it into a large bowl. Add the dissolved coagulant. Using a spoon, stir gently for a few seconds. Let coagulate for 20 minutes.

11 Using a ladle, gently remove as much surface liquid as you can. What's left is the curd.

12 Place a colander over a large bowl. Line the colander with cheesecloth. Pour the curd into the lined bowl. Fold the cheesecloth over the curd to make a bundle. Place a plate directly on top of the bundle and add some weight (one or two canned food items, for example). The heavier the weight and the longer it sits there, the firmer the tofu will be.**** Let drain for at least 30 minutes, removing any liquid from the bowl as needed.

13 Once it is well pressed, place the tofu in a sealed container and cover with fresh water. Store in the fridge for up to 5 days, changing the water every day.

How to Make Soft Tofu

SOAKING	PREPARATION	RESTING TIME	MAKES	KEEPS FOR
8 hours	30 min	1 hour 20 min	4 to 6 servings	3 days in the fridge

MATERIALS
Ramekins or molds
Lids or plastic wrap (to cover the molds)

INGREDIENTS
2 tsp nigari (magnesium chloride)*
4 tsp water
3¼ cups (810 mL) Homemade Soy Beverage**

DIRECTIONS

1 In a bowl, dissolve the nigari (coagulant) in the water. Set aside.

2 In a saucepan over medium heat, bring the soy beverage to a simmer.

3 Remove from the heat. Add the dissolved coagulant. With a spoon, gently stir for a few seconds.

4 Pour the mixture into the ramekins. Allow to set for 20 minutes.

5 Cover the ramekins with plastic wrap and refrigerate for at least 1 hour.

6 Enjoy!

* Nigari is traditionally used as a coagulant for its ability to produce a smoother and silkier texture, but lemon juice also works if you prefer an easier-to-find alternative. Use 2 tbsp lemon juice and omit the water.

** Before you begin, make sure your Homemade Soy Beverage is smooth and pulp-free.

Homemade
Soy Beverage

p. 28

How to Make Smoked Tofu

1   If you have a smoker at home, you can make your own smoked tofu. It's a fairly simple process but it requires a bit of time and preparation. Ideally, choose firm or extra-firm tofu so it can stand up to the smoking process. The tofu must first be drained and pressed to remove as much water as possible. This step is crucial as it allows the tofu to absorb the flavors of the marinade and hold together better during smoking. To remove as much water as you can from your tofu, you can drain it, cut it in cubes and freeze for 24 hours.

2   After thawing, pressing, draining well and drying your tofu, it is recommended that you first let it marinate for at least 1 hour, or even overnight, in a wet marinade of your choice so it develops a stronger flavor.

3   The smoking process usually takes 1 to 2 hours, depending on how intense a flavor you're looking for. During this time, the tofu absorbs the smoke, developing a rich and complex flavor. Please follow the instructions on your individual smoker.

4   Once the smoking is done, let the tofu cool before eating it, or store it in the fridge. Homemade tofu can be eaten as is or used in a wide range of recipes, such as Smoked Tofu Bacon (page 56) or Spicy Korean Tofu Soup (page 148), adding a tasty and unique touch to many dishes.

How to Store Tofu Properly

Here is some advice on how to store different types of tofu properly. Keep in mind that tofu is like a sponge, which means it's sensitive to odors. Because it easily absorbs the flavors around it, avoid storing it near foods with strong odors. If you have tofu that is starting to show signs of deterioration, such as a change in color or smell, it is best to discard it for food safety reasons.

STORING TOFU

TYPE OF TOFU	HOW LONG IT KEEPS	STORING CONDITIONS	HOW OFTEN TO CHANGE THE WATER	FREEZING
Homemade tofu	Eat within 3 to 5 days of making it.	In fresh water, in a sealed container in the fridge	Every day	Cut into portions and blot before placing in a freezer bag. The texture will change slightly after thawing.
Tofu bought in bulk	Eat within 3 to 5 days of buying it.	In fresh water, in a sealed container in the fridge	Every day	Cut into portions and blot before placing in a freezer bag. The texture will change slightly after thawing.
Firm tofu (store-bought)	Eat within 5 to 7 days of opening the package.	In fresh water, in a sealed container in the fridge OR Wrapped in a damp paper towel in a sealable plastic bag	Every day	Cut into portions and blot before placing in a freezer bag. The texture will change slightly after thawing.
Soft and silken tofu (store-bought)	Eat within 2 to 3 days of opening the package.	In the original packaging in the fridge, in a sealable plastic bag	-	Freezing greatly changes the texture of soft tofu and silken tofu; you are therefore advised not to freeze them.

Cooking Tofu More Intuitively

Intuitive cooking is a culinary philosophy that is close to my heart and guides my creativity whenever I'm wearing my apron. This unique approach is based on self-confidence and on the connection to your senses and your own knowledge, whether you are following a recipe or not.

WHAT IS INTUITIVE COOKING?

It's the art of drawing on our knowledge and our senses while preparing a meal, leaving room for spontaneity and creativity.

Intuitive cooking can happen when we're making a simple sandwich or an impromptu breakfast at home. It unfolds when we prepare a pan of vegetables for roasting in the oven without using a recipe. It happens when we choose grapeseed oil instead of olive oil purely by instinct. In short, it's the art of cooking without limits, relying on our own knowledge and preferences.

In our digital age, when online recipes and ready-to-use meal kits are at our fingertips, we risk forgetting to use the know-how and cooking techniques that our ancestors mastered. That's why it's essential to revive these skills, reconnect with culinary traditions and become independent in the kitchen.

THREE CHAPTERS OF BASIC RECIPES

It is in this spirit that I created this book: to offer you the chance to use several recipes intuitively. I got the idea from seeing the readers of my online magazine *La Fraîche* incorporate my Cajun Tofu (page 44) in all kinds of different dishes. I wanted to give you recipes to follow to the letter but also to leave room for your own creativity, starting with certain basics for creating meals that suit you, that you like and that can be adapted to various situations.

The first three chapters are therefore made up of simple and versatile recipes that you can include in dishes you already make, in recipes I offer you later in the book or in dishes you create on the spur of the moment, following your intuition.

- Tofu-based condiments: different sauces that I love to use in cooking plus fully vegan alternatives for some condiments that we use regularly in cooking.
- Multipurpose tofu: seasoned, flavorful and delicious, ready to be eaten as the main protein in a meal or added to your sandwiches, salads, bowls and favorite recipes.
- Tofu in disguise: finger-licking-good plant-based options, all made from tofu, that you can use in place of meat in different dishes.

I hope you will enjoy this way of cooking and that it will allow you to include tofu a little more intuitively on the menu. These recipes are an invitation to explore, innovate and rediscover the pleasure of making unique and delicious meals that reflect your style.

And if your intuition is not taking the lead, I have created for you seven chapters of recipes that you can easily follow, step by step, to make tofu the star of all your meals.

Tofu-Based Condiments

Soft Tofu Sour Cream

PREPARATION	RESTING TIME	MAKES	KEEPS FOR
15 min	1 hour	about 1¼ cups (300 mL)	5 days in the fridge

This vegan sour cream can be used in a wide range of dishes, both savory and sweet: in my Blueberry, Dark Chocolate, Soft Tofu Sour Cream Muffins (page 83), as a base for tzatziki sauce in my Vegan Gyro (page 94), in the Layered Mexican Dip (page 112) and in the Soft Tofu Ranch Dressing, on the next page.

INGREDIENTS

10 oz (300 g) soft tofu
2 tbsp (30 mL) fresh lemon juice
1 tbsp apple cider vinegar
1 tsp salt

DIRECTIONS

1 Drain the soft tofu in a fine-mesh sieve, pressing on it to remove as much liquid as possible.

2 In a blender, combine the drained tofu, lemon juice, vinegar and salt and blend until smooth and creamy.

3 Refrigerate for at least 1 hour before using to allow the flavors to develop.

Soft Tofu Ranch Dressing

PREPARATION	RESTING TIME	MAKES	KEEPS FOR
10 min	1 hour (optional)	about 1 cup (250 mL)	5 days in the fridge

I love ranch dressing: it is versatile and always adds a nice touch of freshness to dishes. This creamy plant-based version is great with raw vegetables as a dip, in a salad like my Barbecued Tofu Salad (page 127), with cauliflower "wings" or as a dip for your favorite chips.

INGREDIENTS

1 cup (250 mL) Soft Tofu Sour
   Cream (page 36)
1 tbsp lemon juice
1 tbsp apple cider vinegar
1 tsp garlic powder
1 tsp onion powder
1 tsp dried chives
1 tsp dried dill
½ tsp salt
¼ tsp pepper

DIRECTIONS

1 In a bowl, using a whisk, combine the sour cream, lemon juice and vinegar until smooth. Add the garlic powder, onion powder, chives, dill, salt and pepper. Mix well until all the ingredients are thoroughly blended.

2 Use right away or let stand in the fridge for at least 1 hour to allow the flavors to develop.

**Soft Tofu
Sour Cream
p. 36**

CONDIMENTS

1 – SOFT TOFU RANCH DRESSING
2 – SOFT TOFU BURGER SAUCE
3 – SOFT TOFU SOUR CREAM
4 – SOFT TOFU VEGAN MAYONNAISE
5 – YUM YUM SAUCE

Soft Tofu Vegan Mayonnaise

PREPARATION	RESTING TIME	MAKES	KEEPS FOR
15 min	1 hour	1¼ cups (300 mL)	5 days in the fridge

Perfect for replacing traditional mayonnaise, this version is completely vegan and lighter. Use it as a condiment for making sauces or for adding directly to your recipes. It will be the base for the other two sauces you will find in this section.

INGREDIENTS

10 oz (300 g) soft tofu
2 tbsp (30 g) Dijon mustard
1 tbsp apple cider vinegar
1 tbsp fresh lemon juice
2 tsp salt
¼ tsp pepper
1 tsp pure maple syrup
3 tbsp (45 mL) olive oil

DIRECTIONS

1 Drain the soft tofu in a fine-mesh sieve, pressing on it to remove as much liquid as possible.

2 In a blender, combine the drained tofu, Dijon mustard, vinegar, lemon juice, salt, pepper and maple syrup. Gradually drizzle the olive oil into the mixture, while blending, until thick and creamy. Adjust the seasoning as needed.

3 Let stand in the fridge for at least 1 hour before using to allow the flavors to develop.

Yum Yum Sauce

PREPARATION	RESTING TIME	MAKES	KEEPS FOR
5 min	1 hour (optional)	about ½ cup (125 mL)	5 days in the fridge

Yum Yum Sauce is a delicious, spicy, creamy sauce from Japan, originally served with seafood dishes, sushi or grilled vegetables. You can use it as a condiment to enhance many vegetarian dishes, like my Salmon-Style Tofu Chirashi (page 143) or Teriyaki Tofu Spring Rolls (page 156).

INGREDIENTS

½ cup (125 mL) Soft Tofu Vegan Mayonnaise (page 39)
2 tbsp (30 g) ketchup
1 tbsp melted butter* of your choice
½ tsp pure maple syrup
½ tsp garlic powder
½ tsp paprika
½ tsp cayenne pepper**
¼ tsp salt
¼ tsp black pepper

DIRECTIONS

1 In a bowl, combine all the ingredients and mix until smooth. Adjust the seasoning as needed.

2 Use right away or let stand in the fridge for at least 1 hour to allow flavors to develop.

* For an entirely vegan recipe, replace the butter with plant-based butter.
** You can increase the quantity of cayenne pepper according to your tolerance level. The original recipe is not too strong and should suit most people.

Soft Tofu Vegan
Mayonnaise

p. 39

Soft Tofu Burger Sauce

PREPARATION	MAKES	KEEPS FOR
5 min	½ cup (125 mL)	5 days in the fridge

The perfect topping for your homemade burgers! I use it in my Fried Chicken–Style Tofu Burger (page 98). It is made with the Soft Tofu Vegan Mayonnaise (page 39), which turns it into a light and delicious option.

INGREDIENTS

¼ cup (60 mL) Soft Tofu Vegan Mayonnaise (page 39)
2 tbsp (30 g) ketchup
1 tbsp prepared mustard
1 tbsp relish
1 tsp hot sauce
½ tsp garlic powder
1 tsp smoked paprika

DIRECTIONS

1 In a bowl, combine all the ingredients and mix until smooth and thoroughly blended.

Soft Tofu Vegan
Mayonnaise

p. 39

Multipurpose Tofu

Cajun Tofu

PREPARATION	COOKING	SERVINGS	KEEPS FOR
5 min	7 to 10 min	3	5 days in the fridge / can be frozen

I couldn't write a tofu cookbook without including the most popular recipe from my online magazine, *La Fraîche*: Cajun Tofu. You'll love it! Many people make it in large quantities for their weekly meal prep and include it in different recipes. In this book, I feature it in Cajun Tofu Sushirritos (page 162) and Cajun Tofu Rigatoni (page 179), but you can also use it as the main protein in a meal, in a salad, in a Buddha bowl, minced in a sandwich, cut into strips in a wrap . . . the possibilities are almost endless! I have also slightly lightened the recipe to make it even more tempting.

INGREDIENTS

1 lb (454 g) extra-firm tofu
2 tbsp (16 g) cornstarch
¼ cup (60 mL) olive oil, divided
1 tbsp Cajun spice mixture
1 tsp salt
¼ cup (15 g) nutritional yeast
2 tbsp (30 g) Dijon mustard
1 tbsp pure maple syrup
¼ cup (60 mL) water

DIRECTIONS

1 In a bowl, break the tofu into pieces (any size) with your hands. Add the cornstarch and mix well.

2 In a skillet over medium-high heat, heat 2 tbsp (30 mL) of the olive oil. Add the tofu and cook, stirring occasionally, until crispy and golden.

3 Meanwhile, in a bowl, combine the remaining 2 tbsp (30 mL) olive oil, Cajun spices, salt, nutritional yeast, Dijon mustard, maple syrup and water and mix until smooth.

4 Pour the mixture into the pan and stir to coat the pieces of tofu well. Cook, stirring, for 1 minute or until the tofu is nice and browned.

5 Serve immediately or let cool and refrigerate.

Balsamic Tofu

PREPARATION	RESTING TIME	COOKING	SERVINGS	KEEPS FOR
5 min	30 min	10 to 15 min	2	5 days in the fridge / can be frozen

In creating this recipe, I had only one thing in mind: place a piece of tofu in the middle of a plate and slice it to eat it* – like we would with a piece of meat. Mission accomplished! Plus, it immediately brings a touch of balsamic flavor to your favorite vegetarian dishes. In this book, it is the featured protein in one of my mason jar salads (page 129) and in my delicious Balsamic Tofu Caprese (page 176).

INGREDIENTS

1 lb (454 g) extra-firm tofu
½ tsp garlic powder
½ tsp pepper
½ tsp salt
1 tsp dried rosemary
2 tbsp (8 g) nutritional yeast
1 tbsp Dijon mustard
¼ cup (60 mL) balsamic vinegar
2 tbsp (30 mL) vegetable oil
2 tbsp (30 mL) pure maple syrup

DIRECTIONS

1 Cut the tofu into 4 equal pieces and place them in a large sealable plastic bag.

2 Add the remaining ingredients, seal and turn the bag until the tofu is well coated. Refrigerate for 30 minutes.

3 In a skillet over medium-high heat, or on a barbecue grill, place the pieces of marinated tofu, one at a time, then pour a little marinade over each piece. Cook for 10 minutes or until the tofu is well browned, turning it halfway through. During cooking, use a brush to baste the tofu pieces regularly with the remaining marinade.

4 Serve immediately or let cool and refrigerate.

* You can serve the tofu pieces whole on a plate or cut them however you like, depending on how you want to use them: sliced, cubed or crumbled.

Mexican-Style Ground Tofu

PREPARATION	COOKING	SERVINGS	KEEPS FOR
15 min	15 min	4	3 days in the fridge / can be frozen

This crumbled tofu is the perfect replacement for traditional Mexican-style ground beef: it is also very good and flavorful! You can use it on nachos, in a salad, in Mexican rice, in my Walking Tofu Tacos recipe (page 123) or in the Layered Mexican Dip recipe (photo on opposite page and recipe on page 112).

INGREDIENTS

1 lb 4 oz (600 g) extra-firm tofu
2 tbsp (30 mL) olive oil
1 red onion, chopped
2 garlic cloves, minced
3 tbsp (24 g) Mexican chili powder
1 tbsp ground cumin
1 tbsp smoked paprika
3 tbsp (45 mL) vegan
  Worcestershire sauce
3 tbsp (51 g) chili sauce
Salt and pepper
Juice of 1 lime

DIRECTIONS

1 In a bowl, crumble the tofu with your hands.

2 In a large skillet over medium heat, heat the oil and sauté the onion for 3 minutes or until transparent. Add the garlic and cook for 2 minutes.

3 Add the crumbled tofu to the pan. Season with the chili powder, cumin, smoked paprika, Worcestershire sauce, chili sauce, and salt and pepper to taste. Cook, stirring frequently, until the tofu is well browned. Remove the pan from the heat.

4 Drizzle the seasoned tofu with lime juice and stir.

5 Serve immediately or let cool and refrigerate.

Teriyaki Tofu

PREPARATION	COOKING	SERVINGS	KEEPS FOR
10 min	20 min	4	5 days in the fridge / can be frozen

Did you know it's really easy to make your own teriyaki sauce? That's why I decided to feature it in this recipe for crispy and umami tofu with its sweet and savory character. You can eat it as is or add it to other dishes, like my mason jar salad (page 128) or Teriyaki Tofu Spring Rolls (page 156).

INGREDIENTS

1 lb 4 oz (600 g) extra-firm tofu, well squeezed
¼ cup (32 g) cornstarch
2 tbsp (30 mL) vegetable oil
Salt and pepper
1 cup (250 mL) water
¼ cup (60 mL) pure maple syrup
¼ cup (60 mL) tamari sauce or soy sauce
2 tbsp (30 mL) seasoned rice vinegar
1 tbsp freshly grated gingerroot
½ tsp garlic powder

DIRECTIONS

1 In a bowl, tear the tofu into strips with your hands. Add the cornstarch and stir to coat the tofu well.

2 In a large skillet over medium-high heat, heat the vegetable oil. Add the tofu strips and salt and pepper to taste. Cook, turning the tofu regularly, for 10 minutes or until browned and crispy.

3 In a bowl, combine the water, maple syrup, tamari sauce, rice vinegar, ginger and garlic powder. Pour the mixture into the skillet and mix well. Bring to a boil, then reduce the heat to low. Simmer for a few minutes, until the sauce is reduced and coats the tofu pieces.

4 Serve immediately or let cool and refrigerate.

Chinese Five-Spice Tofu

PREPARATION	COOKING	SERVINGS	KEEPS FOR
10 min	10 min	4	5 days in the fridge / keep tofu and sauce separate

Generally made with cinnamon, cloves, Szechuan pepper, star anise and fennel, this spice mixture is part of the Chinese culinary tradition – you can easily find it at the supermarket. It makes the sauce for this dish deliciously fragrant, unique and irresistible. Use this recipe as a variation for your General Tso's tofu or in my Five-Spice Tofu Buddha Bowl (page 144).

INGREDIENTS

Tofu
1 lb (454 g) medium-firm tofu
2 tbsp (30 mL) vegetable oil

Sauce
¼ cup (32 g) cornstarch
½ tsp garlic powder
1 tbsp Chinese five-spice powder
1 cup (250 mL) vegetable broth
½ cup (125 mL) tamari sauce or
    soy sauce
¼ cup (60 mL) pure maple syrup
2 tbsp (30 mL) seasoned rice
    vinegar
1 tbsp sriracha sauce

DIRECTIONS

Tofu
1 In a bowl, break the tofu into large chunks with your hands.

2 In a skillet over medium-high heat, heat the vegetable oil and cook the tofu pieces, stirring occasionally, for 5 minutes or until browned. Set aside.

Sauce
3 In a saucepan, off the heat, whisk all the sauce ingredients until well blended.

4 Bring to a boil over medium heat, whisking constantly. As soon as the sauce thickens, remove from the heat.

Assembly
5 Add the tofu to the sauce in the saucepan or pour the sauce directly over the tofu on a plate. If you are not serving it right away, store the tofu and the sauce separately in the fridge.*

* If you keep the sauce and the tofu separate, it will be easier to reheat the sauce. The cornstarch will give the sauce a gelatinous look when it cools, but it will become smooth again when reheated.

Barbecued Tofu

PREPARATION	COOKING	SERVINGS	KEEPS FOR
5 min	15 min	2	5 days in the fridge / can be frozen

In my opinion, this is one of the best recipes to get skeptics to finally like tofu. It's very quick to make, uses only a few ingredients and can be personalized with your favorite barbecue sauce.

INGREDIENTS

1 lb (454 g) extra-firm tofu
2 tbsp (30 mL) olive oil
$\frac{1}{3}$ cup (20 g) nutritional yeast
Salt and pepper
$\frac{1}{2}$ cup (125 g) store-bought
   barbecue sauce

DIRECTIONS

1 In a bowl, break the tofu into any size pieces with your hands.

2 In a large skillet over medium-high heat, combine the olive oil, tofu pieces and nutritional yeast. Add salt and pepper to taste and mix well. Cook for 10 minutes or until the tofu is nicely browned.

3 Add the barbecue sauce and reduce the heat to low, stirring vigorously so the tofu doesn't stick. Cook for 1 to 2 minutes.

4 Serve immediately or let cool and refrigerate.

Mediterranean Tofu

PREPARATION	COOKING	SERVINGS	KEEPS FOR
5 min	15 min	2	3 days in the fridge

I love this recipe! It is quick to prepare, and I always have in the cupboard what I need to make it. You can enjoy it in several ways, such as in my Vegan Gyro (page 94), Mediterranean Pizza (page 117) or Mediterranean Salad (page 139).

INGREDIENTS

1 lb (454 g) medium-firm tofu, cut into strips
2 tbsp (30 mL) olive oil
1 tbsp white balsamic vinegar
$\frac{1}{2}$ tsp garlic powder
1 tsp dried oregano
1 tsp dried basil
1 tbsp cornstarch
Salt and pepper

DIRECTIONS

1 Place all the ingredients in a bowl and stir to coat the tofu well.

2 In a large nonstick skillet over medium-high heat, cook the mixture, turning the tofu strips halfway through, for 10 to 12 minutes or until nicely browned and crispy.

3 Serve immediately or let cool and refrigerate.

Tofu in Disguise

Tofu Feta

PREPARATION	RESTING TIME	MAKES		KEEPS FOR
15 min	1 to 24 hours	about 1 lb/454 g (2 cups/500 mL)		5 days in the fridge

This delicious vegan feta is a great replacement in recipes that use traditional feta. In this book, you'll find it in my Corn Ribs and Tofu Feta with Tex-Mex Sauce (page 119) and in cubes in the Broccoli and Marinated Shallot Salad (page 133). Bonus: you can season the brine to your taste with fresh or dried herbs, or hot pepper flakes, to add a bit of a kick, and even a little olive oil. Don't hesitate to personalize it for garnishing your salads, pasta dishes, pizzas and much more!

INGREDIENTS

1 lb (454 g) extra-firm tofu
2 cups (500 mL) boiling water
2 tbsp (30 mL) lemon juice
2 tbsp (30 mL) apple cider vinegar
¼ cup (15 g) nutritional yeast
1 tbsp sea salt

DIRECTIONS

1 Blot the tofu with a clean towel to remove excess moisture. On a cutting board, cut the tofu into cubes or crumble it. Set aside.

2 In a heatproof sealable container, make the brine by combining the boiling water, lemon juice, vinegar, nutritional yeast and sea salt. Stir until well blended.

3 Immerse the tofu pieces in the prepared brine. Marinate in the fridge for at least 1 hour or, for a more pronounced flavor, up to 24 hours.

Smoked Tofu Bacon

PREPARATION	RESTING TIME	COOKING	SERVINGS	KEEPS FOR
5 min	15 min	16 min	4	5 days in the fridge / can be frozen

This is a new twist on the bacon tofu recipe from my previous book that uses smoked tofu: a success in every way! It's a very simple approach to turning a block of smoked tofu into a pure delight!

INGREDIENTS

3 tbsp (45 mL) pure maple syrup*
2 tbsp (30 mL) tamari sauce or soy sauce*
2 tbsp (33 g) tomato paste
1/4 cup (60 mL) vegetable oil, divided
2 tbsp (8 g) nutritional yeast
1/2 tsp garlic powder
14 oz (400 g) smoked tofu, cut into thin strips

DIRECTIONS

1 In a bowl, make the marinade by combining the maple syrup, tamari sauce, tomato paste, half the vegetable oil, the nutritional yeast and garlic powder and mix until well blended.

2 Place the strips of tofu in a sealable container and pour in the marinade. Seal the container and shake gently to coat the tofu with the marinade. Let stand 15 minutes in the fridge.

3 In a large nonstick skillet over medium-high heat, heat the rest of the vegetable oil and cook the tofu strips (reserving the marinade) for 4 minutes or until browned, turning them halfway through. If needed, cook the strips in several batches to avoid overlap and to ensure uniform cooking.

4 Return all the tofu strips to the pan, add the rest of the marinade and sauté for 1 minute, stirring to coat the tofu well with sauce.

5 Serve immediately or let cool and refrigerate.

* Adjust the quantity of maple syrup and tamari sauce based on your sweet-savory preferences.

Ground Beef–Style Tofu

PREPARATION	COOKING	SERVINGS	KEEPS FOR
10 min	15 min	4	3 days in the fridge / can be frozen

This crumbled tofu is very versatile: it can be used in numerous daily dishes, such as shepherd's pie, stuffed buns and chop suey, or in a pasta sauce, such as Mamie Claire's Long Macaroni with Tomato Sauce (page 184).

INGREDIENTS

2 tbsp (30 mL) vegetable oil
1 yellow onion, finely chopped
1 lb (454 g) extra-firm tofu, crumbled by hand
Salt and pepper
2 tbsp (30 mL) tamari sauce or soy sauce
1 tbsp vegan Worcestershire sauce
1 tsp smoked paprika
½ tsp garlic powder
½ tsp onion powder
2 tbsp (8 g) nutritional yeast

DIRECTIONS

1 In a large skillet over medium heat, heat the oil and sauté the onion for 3 to 4 minutes or until transparent.

2 Add the crumbled tofu and salt and pepper to taste. Cook for 5 to 7 minutes, stirring regularly.

3 Add the tamari sauce, Worcestershire sauce, smoked paprika, garlic powder, onion powder and nutritional yeast. Mix well to coat the tofu evenly with spices.

4 Cook, stirring, for 3 to 4 minutes or until the tofu is the desired texture and color. If needed, adjust the seasoning with salt and pepper.

5 Serve immediately or let cool and refrigerate.

Spicy Sausage Meat–Style Tofu

PREPARATION	COOKING	SERVINGS	KEEPS FOR
15 min	20 min	4	3 days in the fridge / can be frozen

When I was still eating meat, I loved recipes that used spicy sausage meat. Since then, I have managed to find plant-based alternatives on the market that gave me the same wonderful taste, but I wanted to create a homemade version that was less expensive and that I could make quickly, with ingredients I always have on hand. I include this spicy sausage meat–style crumbled tofu in a sandwich (page 101) and in my lasagna (page 170), but you can also use it as a pizza topping or as a filling in baked vegetables with cheese sauce. It's a real treat!

INGREDIENTS

1 tbsp vegetable oil
1 yellow onion, chopped
1 red bell pepper, diced
1 lb (454 g) extra-firm tofu, coarsely
   crumbled with your fingers
Salt and black pepper
2 tbsp (33 g) tomato paste
2 tsp tamari sauce (or soy sauce)
1 tsp vegan Worcestershire sauce
2 tsp pure maple syrup
1 tsp smoked paprika
1 tsp onion powder
1 tsp garlic powder
1 tsp ground cumin
½ tsp chili powder
½ tsp ground coriander
½ tsp cayenne pepper

DIRECTIONS

1 In a large skillet over medium heat, heat the oil and sauté the onion and red pepper for 5 minutes or until tender.

2 Add the crumbled tofu and salt and black pepper to taste. Increase the heat to medium-high. Sauté the tofu, stirring regularly, for 5 minutes or until slightly browned.

3 Add the tomato paste, tamari sauce, Worcestershire sauce, maple syrup, smoked paprika, onion powder, garlic powder, cumin, chili powder, coriander and cayenne pepper. Mix well to coat the tofu evenly with the spices.

4 Cook, stirring frequently, for 5 to 7 minutes or until the tofu is nicely browned and has a texture similar to spicy sausage meat. Adjust the seasoning as needed.

5 Serve immediately or let cool and refrigerate.

Salmon-Style Tofu

PREPARATION	RESTING TIME	COOKING	SERVINGS	KEEPS FOR
15 min	12 to 24 hours	8 min	2	5 days in the fridge

Eat this tofu as if it were a piece of salmon! You can use it on pasta, serve it with rice and vegetables, or make my Salmon-Style Tofu Chirashi with Yum Yum Sauce (page 143).

INGREDIENTS

Marinade
1 cup (250 mL) vegetable broth
1 nori leaf
3 tbsp (45 mL) seasoned rice
  vinegar
2 tsp beetroot powder*
½ tsp ground turmeric
½ tsp garlic powder
1 tsp toasted sesame oil
1 tsp sea salt
1 tsp brown sugar

Tofu
1 lb (454 g) extra-firm tofu
1 nori leaf
2 tbsp (16 g) cornstarch
1 tbsp toasted sesame oil
1 tbsp vegetable oil
Salt and pepper

* You will find beetroot powder in natural food stores and online. Or replace it with a small cooked red beet.
** Before making the notches, you can "carve" the two pieces of tofu into a shape resembling a salmon fillet (see photo on opposite page). Marinate the scraps along with the two pieces.

DIRECTIONS

Marinade
1 In a blender, combine all the marinade ingredients until well blended. Set aside.

Tofu
2 On a cutting board, cut the tofu block in half lengthwise. Make ⅛-inch (3 mm) deep notches diagonally on the surface of the tofu pieces.**

3 Place the tofu pieces in a sealable container and add the marinade. Marinate in the fridge overnight or for up to 24 hours.

4 Remove the tofu pieces from the marinade. Cut the nori leaf so you have two pieces the same size as the tofu pieces. Place 1 piece of nori on the unnotched side of each piece of marinated tofu.

5 Put the cornstarch into a bowl. Add the tofu pieces and turn until well coated.

6 In a skillet over medium-high heat, heat the sesame oil and vegetable oil. Cook the tofu pieces, along with their nori sheets, for 8 minutes, turning them halfway through. Add salt and pepper to taste. Serve immediately or let cool and refrigerate.

Fried Chicken–Style Tofu

PREPARATION	RESTING TIME	COOKING	SERVINGS	KEEPS FOR
30 min	2 hours or up to 24 hours	15 min	4	3 days in the fridge / can be frozen

This recipe is dedicated to my partner, Guillaume. Since he's the biggest fried chicken fan I know, I felt I had to come up with a vegetarian (even vegan!) version of his favorite dish so we could enjoy it together. I serve it as is, with our favorite sauce, at breakfast in my recipe for Waffles and Fried Chicken–Style Tofu (page 73) or in my Fried Chicken–Style Tofu Burger (page 98). Note: even the KFC kid licked his fingers!

INGREDIENTS
Tofu
1 lb (454 g) extra-firm tofu, frozen then thawed*
1 cup (250 mL) unsweetened plain soy beverage
2 tbsp (30 mL) apple cider vinegar
1 tbsp soy sauce (or tamari sauce)
1 tbsp Dijon mustard
1 tbsp vegetable oil
2 tbsp (8 g) nutritional yeast
1 tsp smoked paprika
1 tsp garlic powder
1 tsp onion powder
$\frac{1}{4}$ tsp cayenne pepper
Salt and black pepper

DIRECTIONS
Tofu
1 With your hands, break the tofu block into pieces of your desired size. Set aside.

2 In a sealable container, make the marinade by combining the soy beverage, vinegar, soy sauce, Dijon mustard, oil, nutritional yeast, smoked paprika, garlic powder, onion powder, cayenne pepper, and salt and black pepper to taste.

3 Place the tofu pieces in the marinade. Seal the container and shake gently to coat the tofu with marinade. Let stand at least 2 hours in the fridge or, for more intense flavor, up to 24 hours.

Recipe continues on page 64.

* You can also use a block of fresh tofu that has not been frozen. The texture will be different, and it will absorb a bit less marinade.

INGREDIENTS (continued)
Coating and frying
$\frac{1}{2}$ cup (68 g) all-purpose flour
$\frac{1}{2}$ cup (64 g) cornstarch
1 tbsp baking powder
1 tsp smoked paprika
1 tsp garlic powder
1 tsp onion powder
$\frac{1}{4}$ tsp cayenne pepper
Salt and black pepper
5 cups (1.25 L) canola oil

DIRECTIONS (continued)
Coating and frying
4 In a bowl, make the coating by combining the flour, cornstarch, baking powder, smoked paprika, garlic powder, onion powder, cayenne pepper, and salt and black pepper to taste. Set aside.

5 In a deep fryer or a large, deep saucepan, heat the oil to 350°F (180°C).

6 In a colander over a bowl, drain the tofu pieces and set aside the marinade.

7 Roll the tofu pieces in the coating, covering them completely, then dip them again in the marinade and again in the coating.

8 Fry the tofu pieces, in several batches, in the hot oil for 3 to 4 minutes on each side or until nicely browned and crispy. Drain on sheets of paper towel to remove excess oil.

9 Serve immediately or let cool and refrigerate.**

** Reheat the fried chicken–style tofu in an air fryer to crisp it up again!

Smoked Meat–Style Tofu

PREPARATION	RESTING TIME	COOKING	SERVINGS	KEEPS FOR
15 min	at least 2 hours	10 min	4	3 days in the fridge / can be frozen

Does smoked meat, an iconic Montreal specialty, have a veggie equivalent? The answer is yes, because Dominique Dupuis, a woman I greatly admire, revolutionized the world by launching a range of absolutely decadent ready-to-eat products made with tofu, including a smoked meat–style variety. I tried to honor her (and pay tribute to her!) with my version, which you can make yourself at home. Try it in a sandwich (page 102).

INGREDIENTS

½ tsp ground pepper
½ tsp ground coriander
½ tsp smoked paprika
½ tsp garlic powder
½ tsp onion powder
½ tsp celery seed
¼ tsp dill seed
¼ tsp hot pepper flakes
1 tbsp beetroot powder*
2 tbsp (30 mL) pure maple syrup
2 tbsp (30 mL) tamari sauce
1 tbsp apple cider vinegar
14 oz (400 g) smoked tofu, cut into thin strips
2 tbsp (30 mL) vegetable oil
Salt

DIRECTIONS

1 In a bowl, combine the pepper, coriander, smoked paprika, garlic powder, onion powder, celery seed, dill seed, hot pepper flakes and beetroot powder and mix well.

2 Add the maple syrup, tamari sauce and apple cider vinegar, and mix until the marinade is well blended. Set aside.

3 Place the tofu strips in a sealable plastic bag and add the marinade. Seal the bag and gently massage the tofu to distribute the marinade. Marinate in the fridge for at least 2 hours. The longer it marinates, the more flavor the tofu will have!

4 In a large skillet over medium-high heat, heat the oil. Add the marinated tofu strips (discard the marinade) and spread them out in a single layer. Cook for 3 to 5 minutes on each side, or until nicely browned. Add salt to taste.

5 Serve immediately or let cool and refrigerate.

* You will find beetroot powder in natural food stores and online. Or replace it with a small cooked red beet. In that case, use a blender and process all the marinade ingredients together.

Deli-Style Smoked Tofu Seitan

PREPARATION	COOKING	RESTING TIME	MAKES	KEEPS FOR
15 min	1 hour	8 hours	16 to 20 slices	5 days in the fridge

People often ask me: What can I put in a sandwich when I no longer eat meat? This is where seitan comes in! It's a high-protein paste made by combining spices, condiments and sauces with this key ingredient: vital wheat gluten. Thanks to the gluten, you get a nice texture that resembles meat. By adding smoked tofu, you can make an easy-to-slice seitan that resembles deli meat both for the eyes and for the taste buds! I use it in the Smoked Tofu Seitan Sub (page 97).

INGREDIENTS

14 oz (400 g) smoked tofu, grated
2 cups (240 g) vital wheat gluten*
1 tsp garlic powder
2 tsp onion powder
2 tbsp (30 g) Dijon mustard
3 tbsp (45 g) ketchup
2 tbsp (30 mL) tamari sauce or soy sauce
2 tbsp (30 mL) vegan Worcestershire sauce
2 tbsp (30 mL) vegetable oil
1 tbsp water
Salt and pepper

DIRECTIONS

1 In a large bowl, combine the tofu, wheat gluten, garlic powder, onion powder, Dijon mustard, ketchup, tamari sauce, Worcestershire sauce, oil, water, and salt and pepper to taste until you get a smooth dough.

2 Transfer the dough to a cutting board and knead for 1 to 2 minutes. Form it into a small cylinder or rectangle (your choice).

3 Wrap the seitan log in plastic wrap, sealing the ends like a sausage, so the package is airtight.

4 Bring a large pot filled with water to a boil. Immerse the seitan package in the boiling water and cook over medium-high heat for 1 hour, making sure the water doesn't boil too vigorously.

5 Using tongs, remove the seitan package from the water and let cool. Set aside in the fridge for at least 8 hours or overnight.

6 Gently unwrap the seitan and cut it into thin slices. Serve immediately or store the slices in a sealed container in the fridge.

* You can easily find vital wheat gluten in the organic foods section at the supermarket, in bulk, in natural food stores and online.

Maple Tofu Seitan Roast

PREPARATION	COOKING	RESTING TIME	SERVES	KEEPS FOR
15 min	45 min	8 hours	6 to 8	5 days in the fridge

What's great about making seitan is that you can shape it any way you like. This maple tofu seitan roast, for example: once you slice it, you will love its great texture and delicious maple flavor. It's perfect for brunch, as in my vegetarian croque monsieur recipe (page 81), in a sandwich or as the main protein at suppertime.

INGREDIENTS

Seitan

1 tbsp vegetable oil + some for the pan
12 oz (340 to 375 g) extra-firm tofu
1 cup (120 g) vital wheat gluten*
2 tbsp (16 g) cornstarch
1 tbsp smoked paprika
2 tsp onion powder
1 tsp garlic powder
2 tbsp (8 g) nutritional yeast
3 tbsp (45 mL) pure maple syrup
2 tbsp (30 mL) tamari sauce or soy sauce
1 tbsp tomato paste

Sauce

3 tbsp (45 mL) pure maple syrup
2 tsp Dijon mustard
2 tbsp (30 mL) tamari sauce or soy sauce

* You can easily find wheat gluten in the organic foods section at the supermarket, in bulk, in natural food stores and online.

DIRECTIONS

Seitan

1 Preheat the oven to 350°F (180°C). Grease a baking dish with oil.

2 In a food processor, process the tofu for a few seconds. Add the remaining seitan ingredients and blend until you get a smooth dough.

3 Transfer the dough to a cutting board and knead for 1 to 2 minutes. Shape the dough into a small roast. Using a knife, make diamond-shaped notches on the top. Set aside.

Sauce

4 In a bowl big enough to hold the roast, combine the sauce ingredients and mix until smooth. Place the seitan roast in the sauce and coat thoroughly.

Cooking

5 Transfer the seitan roast to the prepared baking dish and, using a brush, baste it with the sauce. Cover with a lid or aluminum foil and bake for 30 minutes, basting halfway through baking. Remove the lid and baste again, then bake, uncovered, for another 15 minutes.

6 Let the seitan roast cool. Place the roast in a sealed container and refrigerate for at least 8 hours or overnight before cutting into slices and serving.

Morning Dishes

Waffles and Fried Chicken–Style Tofu

PREPARATION	COOKING	SERVINGS	KEEPS FOR
20 min	4 min per waffle	4	3 days in the fridge, separately / can be frozen

INGREDIENTS

1¾ cups (425 mL) plain unsweetened plant-based beverage (soy, almond, oat)
2 tsp lemon juice
2 cups (270 g) all-purpose flour
2 tsp baking powder
¼ tsp fleur de sel
¼ cup (60 mL) grapeseed oil or vegetable oil
¼ cup (60 mL) pure maple syrup
1½ tsp vanilla extract
Vegetable oil (for cooking)

Sides

Fried Chicken–Style Tofu* (page 63)
Pure maple syrup

DIRECTIONS

1 In a bowl, combine the plant-based beverage and lemon juice. Stir and let stand 10 minutes to make "buttermilk." The mixture will curdle; this is normal. Set aside.

2 In a large bowl, combine the flour, baking powder and fleur de sel.

3 Into the "buttermilk" bowl, add the oil, maple syrup and vanilla and mix well.

4 Pour the wet ingredients over the dry ingredients and stir just until blended.

5 Heat a hot waffle iron with a little oil until hot. Pour about ¼ cup (60 mL) waffle batter into the waffle iron. Cook for 4 minutes or until steam stops coming out of the waffle iron and the waffle is nicely browned. Keep warm and continue cooking the rest of the batter the same way.

6 Place the cooked waffles on a large plate and arrange the fried chicken–style tofu around it. Serve with a generous drizzle of maple syrup.

* If you made your fried chicken–style tofu ahead of time, reheat it in an air fryer or in the oven at 450°F (230°C) to crisp it up.

Fried Chicken–Style Tofu

p. 63

Cinnamon Bun–Style Soft Tofu Pancakes

PREPARATION	COOKING	SERVINGS	KEEPS FOR
15 min	20 min	4	3 days in the fridge / the pancakes can be frozen

INGREDIENTS

Pancakes
10 oz (300 g) soft tofu
1 tsp vanilla extract
½ cup (125 mL) unsweetened plain soy beverage
1 cup (135 g) all-purpose flour
2 tbsp (26 g) packed brown sugar
1 tbsp baking powder
½ tsp salt
¼ cup (60 mL) vegetable oil (for cooking), divided

Cinnamon Topping
¼ cup (53 g) packed brown sugar
1 tbsp ground cinnamon
2 tbsp (30 g) butter of your choice, melted

Icing
4 oz (125 g) cream cheese, at room temperature
½ cup (60 g) confectioners' (icing) sugar
½ tsp vanilla extract

* If you like, transfer the cinnamon mixture to a pastry bag or a sealable plastic bag with a corner cut out so you can make a spiral on the surface of the pancake during cooking to create a nice cinnamon bun effect.

DIRECTIONS

Pancakes
1 Drain the soft tofu in a fine-mesh strainer, pressing on it to remove as much liquid as possible.

2 In a blender, combine the soft tofu, vanilla, soy beverage, flour, brown sugar, baking powder and salt. Blend until smooth.

Cinnamon Topping
3 In a small bowl, combine the brown sugar, cinnamon and melted butter. Set aside.*

Cooking
4 Preheat the oven to its lowest temperature.

5 In a skillet over medium heat, heat 1 tbsp oil. Add a small ladle of pancake batter, making a circle shape. Sprinkle generously with the cinnamon topping. When bubbles form on the surface, gently flip the pancake and cook the other side until nicely browned.

6 Repeat the process with the rest of the oil and the batter. Keep the cooked pancakes warm in the preheated oven.

Icing
7 In a bowl, using an electric mixer, beat the cream cheese, confectioners' sugar and vanilla until creamy.

8 Top the pancakes with icing and serve right away.

Overnight Soft Tofu Oats

PREPARATION	RESTING TIME	SERVINGS	KEEPS FOR
10 min	at least 6 hours	2	2 days

I love overnight oats! They are perfect for eating on the go, and this recipe is no exception. Thanks to the soft tofu, it is high in vegetable protein, which means you can enjoy a nutritious breakfast that will stay with you.

INGREDIENTS

5 oz (150 g) soft tofu
1 cup (95 g) quick-cooking rolled oats
2 tbsp (30 mL) pure maple syrup
½ cup (125 mL) unsweetened plain soy beverage
½ tsp vanilla extract
1 pinch of salt
½ cup (70 g) soft fresh fruits (strawberries, blueberries, raspberries, etc.)
2 tbsp (10 g) slivered almonds
1 tbsp chia seeds

DIRECTIONS

1 In a blender, combine the soft tofu, oats, maple syrup, soy beverage, vanilla and salt until creamy and smooth.

2 Divide the mixture into two pint (500 mL) mason jars. Place the fruit, almonds and chia seeds on top.

3 Tightly seal the jars and refrigerate for at least 6 hours, preferably overnight.

4 Enjoy in the morning!

Chantal's Egg-Style Tofu Vegetable Bites

PREPARATION	COOKING	SERVINGS	KEEPS FOR
10 min	35 min	6 large or 12 small	5 days in the fridge / can be frozen

This recipe is a stroke of genius from my friend Chantal. In addition to being the magician behind the splendor of the photos of the recipes in this book, she was my partner in crime in the kitchen while I prepared them. I wanted to create a breakfast recipe that would allow you to use up any less-than-perfect vegetables and would call to mind an omelet, a frittata or mini quiches, but without eggs. At that moment, Chantal pointed to her muffin pan and said: "I've got it! Egg-style tofu bites!" Enjoy every bite of this yummy breakfast treat!

INGREDIENTS

1 lb (454 g) medium-firm tofu
¼ cup (60 mL) unsweetened plain soy beverage
2 tbsp (8 g) nutritional yeast
1 tbsp cornstarch
½ tsp black salt (kala namak)
1 tsp ground turmeric
Pepper
2 tbsp (30 mL) vegetable oil
1 cup (250 mL) diced vegetables of your choice for the filling (tomatoes, onions, spinach, mushrooms, bell peppers, etc.)

DIRECTIONS

1 Preheat the oven to 375°F (190°C). Place a rack in the middle of the oven. Place paper or silicone liners in a pan for 6 large or 12 small muffins, or lightly grease each mold.

2 In a bowl, crumble the tofu with your hands. Add the soy beverage, nutritional yeast, cornstarch, black salt, turmeric and pepper to taste. Mix well. Set aside.

3 In a nonstick skillet over medium heat, heat the oil and cook the vegetables for a few minutes, until tender.

4 Add the cooked vegetables to the tofu mixture. Mix well.

5 Fill the muffin cups equally with the mixture.

6 Bake for 30 minutes, until set and heated through.

7 Let cool 4 to 5 minutes before eating.

Maple Tofu Seitan Croque Monsieur

PREPARATION
20 min

COOKING
20 min

SERVINGS
4

INGREDIENTS

3 tbsp (45 g) your choice of butter*
  + some for the bread
3 tbsp (24 g) all-purpose flour
1 cup (250 mL) milk or unsweetened
  plain soy beverage
Salt and pepper
8 slices of crusty bread
1 Maple Tofu Seitan Roast, sliced
  thinly (page 69)
2½ cups (280 g) grated cheddar
  cheese*

DIRECTIONS

1 Preheat the oven to 400°F (200°C). Line a baking sheet with parchment paper.

2 Make the béchamel sauce. In a saucepan over medium heat, melt 3 tbsp (45 g) butter. Add the flour and whisk for 1 minute. Add the milk, whisking constantly. Season with salt and pepper to taste. Remove from the heat when the mixture has thickened. Set aside.

3 Place 4 slices of bread on the prepared baking sheet and butter them. Pour ¼ cup (60 mL) béchamel sauce over each one. Cover each with a few slices of maple tofu seitan roast and top with half the cheese. Close up the croque monsieurs with the other 4 slices of bread and top each with the remaining cheese.

4 Bake for 10 to 12 minutes, or until the cheese is nicely browned.

5 Serve immediately.

* You can use plant-based butter and dairy-free cheddar-style cheese to make the recipe vegan.

**Maple Tofu
Seitan Roast**

p. 69

Scrambled Tofu

PREPARATION	COOKING	SERVINGS	KEEPS FOR
15 min	10 min	3	3 days in the fridge / can be frozen

A classic breakfast dish in vegan cuisine, this scrambled tofu is very tasty thanks to its secret ingredient: black salt, or kala namak. Because of its high sulfur content, this salt gives foods the flavor of cooked egg. You can easily find it in natural food stores and online. You can also omit it; the result will still look like scrambled eggs but will not taste as much like them. I also use this recipe as the base for the very tasty Scrambled Tofu Sandwiches (page 93).

INGREDIENTS
1 lb (454 g) medium-firm tofu
2 tbsp (30 mL) vegetable oil
1 tsp ground turmeric
½ tsp paprika
½ tsp ground cumin
½ tsp black salt (kala namak)
2 tbsp (8 g) nutritional yeast
Pepper
1 tbsp chopped fresh chives

DIRECTIONS
1 Gently press the tofu in a clean towel to remove excess water.

2 In a large skillet over medium heat, heat the oil. Crumble the tofu directly into the pan with your hands to get a texture like that of scrambled eggs.

3 Add the turmeric, paprika, cumin, black salt and nutritional yeast. Season with pepper to taste and mix well. Cook the tofu, stirring occasionally, for 5 minutes or until hot.

4 Remove from the heat. Garnish with chives and serve immediately.

Photo on page 84.

Blueberry, Dark Chocolate and Soft Tofu Sour Cream Muffins

PREPARATION
15 min

COOKING
20 to 25 min

MAKES
12 muffins

KEEPS FOR
1 day at room temperature / 5 days
in the fridge / can be frozen

INGREDIENTS

2 cups (270 g) all-purpose flour
1 tbsp baking powder
1 tsp baking soda
1 tsp salt
1 cup (250 mL) Soft Tofu Sour
  Cream (page 36)
¼ cup (60 mL) pure maple syrup
½ cup (125 mL) unsweetened plain
  soy beverage
¼ cup (60 mL) vegetable oil
1 tsp vanilla extract
1 cup (150 g) fresh or frozen
  blueberries
½ cup (85 g) semi-sweet chocolate
  chips

DIRECTIONS

1 Preheat the oven to 400°F (200°C). Place a rack in the middle of the oven. Place paper or silicone liners in a 12-cup muffin pan, or lightly grease each mold.

2 In a large bowl, combine the flour, baking powder, baking soda and salt. Set aside.

3 In another bowl, whisk together the soft tofu sour cream, maple syrup, soy beverage, oil and vanilla until smooth.

4 Pour the liquid ingredients over the dry ingredients and mix gently.

5 Add the blueberries and chocolate chips and mix gently until blended.

6 Fill the muffin cups two-thirds full.

7 Bake for 5 minutes. Lower the temperature to 350°F (180°C)* and continue baking for 15 to 20 minutes or until a toothpick inserted in the center of a muffin comes out clean.

8 Let cool for about 10 minutes before eating.

Photo on page 84.

* Baking for 5 minutes at 400°F (200°C) and then continuing to bake at 350°F (180°C) allows the muffins to rise nicely and form spectacular tops!

**Soft Tofu
Sour Cream

p. 36**

Smoked Tofu and Market Vegetable Quiche

PREPARATION	RESTING TIME	COOKING	SERVINGS	KEEPS FOR
30 min	2 hours	50 min	6	5 days in the fridge / can be frozen

INGREDIENTS

Short crust pastry*

1 cup (135 g) all-purpose flour
½ cup (114 g) cold unsalted butter or plant-based butter, grated**
2½ tbsp (37 mL) cold water
½ tsp white vinegar
1 pinch of salt

DIRECTIONS

Short crust pastry

1 In a large bowl, combine the flour and cold butter. Blend the butter into the flour with your fingers or a pastry blender. Set aside.

2 In a bowl, combine the cold water, vinegar and salt. Add it to the flour mixture and blend with your hands until a ball of dough forms.

3 Wrap the dough in plastic wrap or place it in a sealed container. Let rest in the fridge for at least 2 hours.

* In a hurry? Use store-bought short crust pastry!
** You read that right: we grate the butter when it's cold. Pro tip!

Quiche

1 tsp melted butter, cooled
2 tbsp (30 mL) olive oil
1 red onion, chopped
Florets from 1 head of broccoli, cut
   in pieces (about 1½ cups/135 g)
2 zucchini, cut in thin rounds
   (around 190 g/1½ cups)
6 oz (175 g) smoked tofu, diced
12 cherry tomatoes, halved
4 beaten eggs
1 cup (250 mL) milk or unsweetened
   plain soy beverage
½ cup (75 g) crumbled Tofu Feta
   (page 55) or your choice of feta
½ cup (55 g) grated cheddar
   cheese***
1 tbsp Dijon mustard
1 tsp paprika
1 tbsp chopped fresh parsley
1 tbsp chopped fresh basil
Salt and pepper

Quiche

4 Preheat the oven to 375°F (190°C). Grease a 10-inch (25 cm) pie plate with the melted butter.

5 In a large saucepan over medium-high heat, heat the oil and cook the onion, broccoli, zucchini and smoked tofu for 5 to 10 minutes or until the tofu is browned, stirring occasionally. Remove from the heat and set aside in a bowl. Mix in the cherry tomatoes.

6 In a large bowl, combine the beaten eggs, milk, tofu feta, cheddar, Dijon mustard, paprika, parsley and basil, and season with salt and pepper to taste. Set aside.

7 Roll out the pastry on a floured surface and line the prepared pie plate with the rolled out dough. Distribute the vegetable mixture and tofu evenly on the pastry. Pour the egg mixture over the top.

8 Bake for 40 minutes, until the egg is set.

9 Let the quiche cool slightly before eating.

Photo on page 85.

*** Use dairy-free cheddar-style
   cheese to make the recipe vegan.

Tofu Feta

p. 55

Let's Hear It for Sandwiches!

Tofu, Lettuce and Tomato (TLT) Tortillas

PREPARATION	COOKING	MAKES	KEEPS FOR
10 min	6 to 8 min	4 tortillas	1 to 2 days in the fridge

I'm sure you've seen this tortilla-folding technique on social media. I couldn't help making an original version, my "TLT," with tofu, lettuce and tomato. A sure-fire hit!

INGREDIENTS

4 large whole wheat tortillas
12 slices Smoked Tofu Bacon (page 56)
¼ head iceberg lettuce, finely chopped
½ cup (125 mL) Soft Tofu Vegan Mayonnaise (page 39) or your choice of mayonnaise
2 medium tomatoes, sliced

DIRECTIONS

1 Place the 4 tortillas on a cutting board. Using a knife, cut a straight line from the center of each tortilla to the bottom edge.

2 In the lower-left section of each tortilla, arrange 3 slices of tofu bacon.

3 In the upper-left section of each tortilla, place 1 portion of lettuce.

4 On the upper-right section of each tortilla, spread 2 tbsp (30 mL) mayonnaise and add the tomato slices.

5 Fold the remaining lower-right section of each tortilla over the mayonnaise and tomatoes. Next, fold left to cover the lettuce. Finally, fold down to cover the tofu bacon topping.

6 In a skillet over medium heat, toast the wraps for 6 to 8 minutes or until the tortillas become crispy and the tofu bacon is hot, turning them halfway through.

7 Serve right away.

Smoked Tofu Bacon

p. 56

Soft Tofu Vegan Mayonnaise

p. 39

Scrambled Tofu Sandwiches

PREPARATION	RESTING TIME	SERVINGS	KEEPS FOR
10 min	30 min	4	5 days in the fridge (for the mixture)

INGREDIENTS
1 recipe Scrambled Tofu (page 82)
3 tbsp (45 mL) Soft Tofu Vegan
   Mayonnaise (page 39) or your
   choice of mayonnaise
2 tbsp (30 g) Dijon mustard
2 tbsp (16 g) finely chopped red
   onion
2 tbsp (6 g) chopped fresh chives
Salt and pepper
8 small sandwich rolls

DIRECTIONS
1 Make the scrambled tofu if it's not already made. Let cool at room temperature or in the fridge before using.

2 Using a fork, crumble the scrambled tofu into a bowl. Add the mayonnaise, Dijon mustard, onion and chives. Season with salt and pepper to taste and stir.

3 Transfer the mixture to a sealed container. Refrigerate for at least 30 minutes to allow the flavors to develop.

4 Fill the 8 rolls equally with the mixture and enjoy.

Scrambled Tofu

p. 82

Soft Tofu Vegan
Mayonnaise

p. 39

Vegan Gyro with Tzatziki

PREPARATION	COOKING	MAKES
15 min	10 min	4 gyros

INGREDIENTS

Tzatziki

½ cup (125 mL) Soft Tofu Sour Cream (page 36) or your choice of sour cream

2 garlic cloves, finely grated

1 Lebanese cucumber or ½ English cucumber, diced

1 tbsp chopped fresh mint

Salt and pepper

Gyros

4 pita breads

1 tbsp vegetable oil (optional)

½ head romaine lettuce, finely chopped (about 2 cups/100 g)

1 red onion, cut in strips

2 tomatoes, sliced

1 recipe Mediterranean Tofu (page 51)

DIRECTIONS

Tzatziki

1 In a bowl, combine the sour cream, garlic, cucumber and mint. Season with salt and pepper to taste. Set aside in the fridge.

Gyros

2 If desired, heat the pita breads. In a large skillet over medium heat, heat the oil and toast the pitas, turning them halfway through, for 4 minutes or until lightly toasted.

3 Evenly spread the tzatziki on each hot pita. Top each with lettuce, red onion, tomato and Mediterranean tofu. Fold the pitas in half to make the gyros.

4 Serve right away.

Soft Tofu Sour Cream

p. 36

Mediterranean Tofu

p. 51

Smoked Tofu Seitan Sub

PREPARATION	COOKING	MAKES
20 min	5 min	4 subs

INGREDIENTS

4 submarine buns
¼ cup (60 mL) Soft Tofu Vegan Mayonnaise (page 39) or your choice of mayonnaise
¼ cup (60 g) Dijon mustard
2 tbsp (30 mL) apple cider vinegar
2 tbsp (30 mL) pure maple syrup
Salt and pepper
16 slices Deli-Style Smoked Tofu Seitan (page 66)
¼ head iceberg lettuce, finely chopped
2 tomatoes, sliced
½ English cucumber, cut in rounds
½ red onion, sliced finely
1 green bell pepper, sliced finely
¼ cup (35 g) sliced pickles

DIRECTIONS

1 Preheat the oven to 350°F (180°C). Toast the buns on the middle rack for 5 minutes or until slightly crusty. Remove the buns from oven and cut in half.

2 Meanwhile, in a small bowl, combine the mayonnaise, Dijon mustard, apple cider vinegar and maple syrup. Season with salt and pepper to taste. Spread the sauce on the toasted buns.

3 Assemble the subs by placing 4 slices of smoked tofu seitan on the bottom half of each bun. Equally distribute the lettuce, tomatoes, cucumber, onion, green pepper and pickles on each bun, and place the top half of the bun on each sub.

4 Serve right away.

Soft Tofu Vegan
Mayonnaise

p. 39

Deli-Style Smoked
Tofu Seitan

p. 66

Fried Chicken–Style Tofu Burger

PREPARATION
20 min

COOKING
5 to 10 min

MAKES
4 burgers

I've been dreaming of this burger for years! A gourmet delight, great texture, full of flavor and 100% vegan.

INGREDIENTS

4 hamburger buns, halved
1 tbsp vegetable oil (optional)
¼ cup (60 mL) Soft Tofu Burger Sauce (page 41)
2 cups (180 g) chopped red cabbage
1 recipe Fried Chicken–Style Tofu* (page 63)
2 dill pickles, sliced lengthwise

DIRECTIONS

1 If desired, toast the buns. In a large skillet over medium heat, heat the oil and place the buns cut-side down. Toast for 4 minutes or until golden.

2 Assemble the burgers by spreading 1 tbsp burger sauce on the bottom half of each bun, then add the cabbage, fried chicken–style tofu and pickles. Place the top half of the bun on each burger.

3 Serve right away.

* If you made your Fried Chicken–Style Tofu ahead of time, reheat it in an air fryer or in the oven at 450°F (230°C) to crisp it up.

Soft Tofu
Burger Sauce

p. 41

Fried Chicken–
Style Tofu

p. 63

Spicy Sausage Meat–Style Tofu Sandwich

PREPARATION	COOKING	MAKES
15 min	12 min	4 sandwiches

INGREDIENTS

2 tbsp (30 mL) olive oil
1 green bell pepper, cut in strips
1 red bell pepper, cut in strips
$\frac{1}{2}$ red onion, cut in strips
1 recipe Spicy Sausage Meat–Style
   Tofu (page 59)
1 tsp dried oregano
1 tsp dried basil
Salt and pepper
2 cups (500 mL) store-bought
   marinara sauce
4 small baguettes
$1\frac{1}{2}$ cups (168 g) grated mozzarella
   cheese*
15 to 20 fresh basil leaves

DIRECTIONS

1 In a skillet over medium heat, heat the oil and sauté the peppers, onion, spicy sausage meat–style tofu, oregano and basil for 5 to 7 minutes or until the vegetables are tender. Season with salt and pepper to taste.

2 Add the marinara sauce, stir and simmer for a few minutes, until hot.

3 Meanwhile, cut the baguettes in half lengthwise.

4 Assemble the sandwiches by spreading the sausage meat-style tofu mixture on the bottom halves of the baguettes. Add the mozzarella and basil leaves to the sandwiches and close them up with the tops of the baguettes.

5 Serve right away.

* Use dairy-free mozzarella-style cheese to make the recipe vegan.

Spicy Sausage
Meat–Style Tofu

p. 59

Smoked Meat–Style Tofu Sandwich

PREPARATION
15 min

COOKING
10 min

MAKES
4 sandwiches

INGREDIENTS
1 recipe Smoked Meat–Style Tofu
  (page 65)
½ cup (125 mL) prepared mustard
1 small red onion, finely chopped
  (around ½ cup/65 g)
8 slices rye bread
2 dill pickles, sliced

DIRECTIONS
1 In a skillet over medium heat, cook the tofu strips for 2 minutes on each side or until hot. Set aside.

2 In a small bowl, combine the mustard and onion.

3 Assemble the sandwiches by spreading 1 tbsp mustard mixture on each slice of rye bread. Distribute the tofu slices and dill pickles on 4 slices of bread. Close up the sandwiches with the remaining slices.

4 Serve right away.

Smoked
Meat–Style Tofu
p. 65

Enjoy in Good Company

Mexican Quinoa

PREPARATION	COOKING	SERVINGS	KEEPS FOR
15 min	15 min	4	5 days in the fridge

INGREDIENTS

1 cup (180 g) quinoa
1⅔ cups (400 mL) water
1 tbsp canola oil
1 recipe Mexican-Style Ground Tofu
   (page 46)
1 cup (180 g) diced seeded fresh
   tomatoes
1 can (14 oz/398 mL) black beans,
   drained and rinsed
1 cup (133 g) corn kernels
Salt and pepper'

Toppings

Chopped fresh cilantro leaves
Lime juice
Soft Tofu Sour Cream (page 36) or
   your choice of sour cream
Grated cheese*
Salsa

DIRECTIONS

1 Place the quinoa in a saucepan and add the water. Add salt to taste and bring to a boil over high heat. Turn the heat to low, cover and cook for 12 minutes. Remove from the heat and set aside.

2 In a large skillet over medium heat, heat the oil and sauté the Mexican-style ground tofu and tomatoes for 2 minutes. Add the cooked quinoa, black beans and corn kernels. Add salt and pepper to taste, and stir. Cook for 2 to 3 minutes.

3 Serve in bowls and garnish to taste with cilantro leaves, lime juice, soft tofu sour cream, grated cheese and/or salsa.

* Use grated dairy-free cheese or omit the cheese to make the recipe vegan.

Mexican-Style
Ground Tofu

p. 46

Soft Tofu
Sour Cream

p. 36

Tofu Skewers with Cranberry Barbecue Sauce

PREPARATION	COOKING	MAKES	KEEPS FOR
15 min	20 to 30 min	6 skewers	5 days in the fridge / can be frozen

INGREDIENTS

1 lb 4 oz (600 g) extra-firm tofu
3 tbsp (45 mL) olive oil, divided
Salt and pepper
1 shallot, chopped
2 garlic cloves, finely chopped
½ cup (50 g) fresh or thawed
   cranberries, coarsely chopped
1 tbsp smoked paprika
¼ cup (60 mL) vegan
   Worcestershire sauce
1 cup (240 g) ketchup
2 tbsp (30 mL) red wine vinegar
¼ cup (60 g) Dijon mustard
¼ cup (60 mL) pure maple syrup

Suggested sides

Seasonal vegetables, grilled or
   cooked in aluminum foil or
   parchment paper

DIRECTIONS

1 Soak six long wood skewers in water for 30 minutes.

2 Cut the tofu into large cubes, all the same size. Slide the tofu cubes onto the skewers. Using a brush, baste the cubes with 2 tbsp (30 mL) oil. Add salt and pepper to taste, and set aside.

3 In a cast iron skillet on a barbecue grill, or in a saucepan on the stove over medium heat, add the remaining 1 tbsp oil, the shallot, garlic and cranberries. Cook for 5 minutes or until the cranberries are soft. Add the smoked paprika, Worcestershire sauce, ketchup, red wine vinegar, Dijon mustard and maple syrup. Bring to a boil and cook for 5 minutes, stirring occasionally so the sauce doesn't stick. Remove the sauce from the heat.

4 On a barbecue grill or in a large skillet on the stove over high heat, cook the tofu skewers, turning them halfway through, for 12 minutes or until nicely browned on each side. With a brush, baste the skewers with sauce on one side and cook for 2 or 3 minutes. Turn the skewers, baste again, and cook for another 2 to 3 minutes.

5 Serve right away.

Layered Mexican Dip

PREPARATION	SERVINGS	KEEPS FOR
15 min	about 8	2 days in the fridge

This has been a classic holiday recipe on my dad's side of the family for many years. Suddenly, it's trendy! I decided to make my version even more tempting using my Mexican-Style Tofu (page 46). It's also an excellent way to enjoy the Soft Tofu Sour Cream (page 36), making the recipe more nutritious and a bit lighter.

INGREDIENTS

1 cup (250 mL) Soft Tofu Sour Cream (page 36) or your choice of sour cream
8 oz (250 g) cream cheese, softened
1$\frac{1}{2}$ cups (375 mL) store-bought salsa
$\frac{1}{2}$ recipe Mexican-Style Ground Tofu (page 46)
1 cup (112 g) grated cheddar cheese or a mixture of Mexican cheese
1 tomato, seeded and diced
1 jalapeño pepper, finely chopped (optional)
3 green onions, chopped
Tortilla chips or corn chips

DIRECTIONS

1 In a large bowl, combine the sour cream and cream cheese and mix until creamy and smooth. Spread out the mixture evenly in a transparent serving dish or deep plate.

2 Evenly spread the salsa on the cream cheese mixture. Add the Mexican-style ground tofu and spread it out over the salsa. Sprinkle with cheese and dot with diced tomato, jalapeño pepper, if desired, and green onions.

3 Serve with tortilla chips or corn chips.

Photos on pages 47 and 111.

Soft Tofu
Sour Cream

p. 36

Mexican -Style
Ground Tofu

p. 46

Garlic and Chive Tofu Spread

PREPARATION	RESTING TIME	SERVINGS	KEEPS FOR
10 min	1 hour	6	5 days in the fridge

I love spreads and dips, especially when they are nutritious and packed with flavor. You can enjoy this one with fresh vegetables or crackers or use it as a substitute for mayonnaise to spread on sandwiches.

INGREDIENTS

1 lb (454 g) medium-firm tofu, coarsely crumbled with your fingers
2 tbsp (30 mL) olive oil
2 garlic cloves
2 tbsp (6 g) chopped fresh chives
2 tbsp (8 g) nutritional yeast
2 tbsp (30 mL) lemon juice
$\frac{1}{2}$ tsp onion powder
Salt and pepper

DIRECTIONS

1 In a food processor, combine the tofu, olive oil, garlic, chives, nutritional yeast, lemon juice and onion powder and blend until smooth and creamy. Season with salt and pepper to taste and blend well. Stop the machine to scrape the sides of the bowl and mix well, if needed. Taste and adjust the seasoning, if needed.

2 Transfer the tofu spread to a sealable container and refrigerate for at least 1 hour before serving.

Photo on page 114.

Spicy Tofu and Cheese Croquettes

PREPARATION	FRYING	MAKES	KEEPS FOR
20 min	12 min	24	5 days in the fridge / can be frozen

This recipe is one of my best friend Camille's favorites. She loves it so much, she makes it several times a month and has everyone try it! It's the type of recipe where the tofu goes unnoticed, which allows people to befriend it more easily and enjoy it.

INGREDIENTS

1 lb (454 g) extra-firm tofu, grated
1½ cups (168 g) grated mozzarella cheese
2 beaten eggs
2 cups (120 g) panko breadcrumbs, divided
Salt and pepper
¾ cup (100 g) all-purpose flour
¾ cup (175 mL) unsweetened plain soy beverage
2 tbsp (30 mL) lemon juice
½ tsp onion powder
½ tsp smoked paprika
5 cups (1.25 L) canola oil
½ cup (125 mL) hot sauce
⅓ cup (113 g) liquid honey

DIRECTIONS

1 In a large bowl, combine the tofu, mozzarella, eggs and 1 cup (60 g) panko breadcrumbs. Season with salt and pepper, and mix well. With your hands, roll the mixture into 24 balls. Set aside on a large plate.

2 In one bowl, place the flour. In a second bowl, mix together the soy beverage and lemon juice. In a third bowl, mix together the remaining panko breadcrumbs, onion powder and smoked paprika. Season with salt and pepper to taste, and stir.

3 Roll the croquettes one at a time first in the flour, then dip them in the soy beverage mixture, and finally coat them in the panko mixture.

4 In a deep fryer or large, deep saucepan, heat the canola oil to 350°F (180°C). Fry the croquettes in batches of 8, turning them halfway through, for 4 minutes or until brown and crispy. Using a slotted spoon, transfer the fried croquettes to a paper towel to absorb the excess oil.

5 Into a large serving bowl, mix the hot sauce and honey. Add the fried croquettes and stir until well coated in sauce.

6 Serve right away.

Photo on page 115.

Mediterranean Pizza

PREPARATION	COOKING	MAKES	KEEPS FOR
15 min	30 to 35 min	4 slices	2 days in the fridge

INGREDIENTS

½ red bell pepper, cut in strips
½ cup (75 g) cherry tomatoes, halved
½ red onion, cut in thin strips
½ tsp hot pepper flakes
2 tbsp (30 mL) olive oil, divided
Salt and pepper
Dough for 1 pizza crust (store-bought or homemade)
½ recipe Mediterranean Tofu (page 51)
½ cup (85 g) quartered drained marinated artichokes

Toppings

Fresh oregano leaves
Buffalo mozzarella cheese, sliced*
Drizzle of pure maple syrup

DIRECTIONS

1 Preheat the oven to 450°F (230°C). Line a baking sheet with parchment paper. If you use a pizza stone, put it in the oven to preheat. If not, cover a second baking sheet with parchment paper.

2 In a bowl, combine the red pepper, cherry tomatoes, red onion, hot pepper flakes and 1 tbsp olive oil and mix well. Season with salt and pepper to taste. Spread the mixture on the prepared baking sheet. Bake for 15 to 20 minutes or until the vegetables are golden and roasted.

3 On a floured work surface, roll out the pizza dough. Spread the roasted vegetable mixture on the dough. Add the Mediterranean tofu strips and artichoke quarters. Drizzle on the remaining olive oil.

4 Transfer the pizza to the preheated pizza stone or the other prepared baking sheet and bake for 12 to 15 minutes or until the crust is golden and crispy.

5 Garnish with fresh oregano leaves, buffalo mozzarella and a drizzle of maple syrup.

6 Let the pizza rest a few minutes before cutting into slices and serving.

Photo on page 115.

* Use dairy-free cheese or omit the cheese to make the recipe vegan.

Mediterranean Tofu p. 51

Corn Ribs and Tofu Feta with Tex-Mex Sauce

PREPARATION	COOKING	SERVINGS	KEEPS FOR
15 min	32 min	4	3 days in the fridge

During a family corn roast, my dad, with my cousin Antoine's help, made corn cob ribs just for fun without really following a recipe. They're called "ribs" because of the shape but also because you gnaw right on the cob, a little like people do with meat on the bone. So delicious! I vowed to come up with my own recipe so I could eat it every day during corn season!

INGREDIENTS

Tex-Mex sauce
1 cup (250 g) plain Greek yogurt*
1 tbsp lemon juice
1 tsp ground cumin
1 tsp chili powder
1/2 tsp smoked paprika
Salt and pepper

Corn ribs
3 tbsp (45 g) melted butter*
1 tbsp tomato paste
1/2 tsp dry mustard
1 tsp brown sugar
1/2 tsp chili powder
1/4 tsp onion powder
1/4 tsp garlic powder
1/2 tsp smoked paprika
3 tbsp (45 mL) olive oil
4 ears of corn, cut into four
    pieces lengthwise**

Toppings
Tofu Feta, crumbled (page 55)
Chopped fresh parsley

Tofu Feta

p. 55

DIRECTIONS

Tex-Mex sauce

1 In a bowl, combine the yogurt, lemon juice, cumin, chili powder and smoked paprika and mix well. Season with salt and pepper to taste. Set aside in the fridge.

Corn ribs

2 Preheat the oven to 375°F (190°C). Line a baking sheet with parchment paper.

3 In a large bowl, combine the melted butter, tomato paste, dry mustard, brown sugar, chili powder, onion powder, garlic powder, smoked paprika and oil and mix well. Place the quartered cobs in the bowl, stir to coat the corn ribs in the mixture and place them on the prepared baking sheet.

4 Bake the corn for 30 minutes or until nicely browned, turning them halfway through.

5 Turn on the oven broiler and broil the corn for 2 minutes to make them slightly crispy.

6 Place the corn ribs on a serving plate and garnish generously with tofu feta and parsley. Serve right away with Tex-Mex sauce on the side.

* Use plant-based yogurt and butter to make the recipe vegan.
** Cutting the cobs requires a lot of strength and a sharp knife. You can put the cobs in a large pan of water and microwave them for 2 to 3 minutes to soften them a little before cutting.

Tofu Polpette with Tomato Sauce

PREPARATION	COOKING	MAKES	KEEPS FOR
20 min	35 min	about 16 polpette	3 to 4 days in the fridge / can be frozen

Polpette are an Italian cuisine classic that can be served as an appetizer or a main dish. Polpette is the plural of polpetta, which means "ball." In Italy, these balls can be made with meat, vegetables or fish. We say you can also make them with tofu! Serve them with a simple tomato sauce or on their own, with hot bread or on pasta.

INGREDIENTS

Tomato sauce

2 tbsp (30 mL) olive oil
1 onion, chopped
2 garlic cloves, chopped
1 can (14 oz/398 mL) crushed
  tomatoes
½ cup (125 mL) water
1 tsp dried oregano
1 tsp pure maple syrup
Salt and pepper

Polpette

1 lb (454 g) medium-firm tofu, well
  pressed
½ cup (25 g) grated parmesan
  cheese
2 eggs, beaten
1 yellow onion, finely chopped
2 garlic cloves, chopped
¾ cup (84 g) Italian-style
  breadcrumbs
1 tbsp tamari sauce or soy sauce
1 tbsp olive oil
1 tbsp chopped fresh parsley
1 tsp dried oregano
½ tsp dried basil
Salt and pepper
3 tbsp (45 mL) vegetable oil

DIRECTIONS

Tomato sauce

1 In a large saucepan over medium heat, heat the olive oil and sauté the onion for 2 minutes or until transparent. Add the garlic and cook for 1 minute. Add the crushed tomatoes, water, oregano and maple syrup. Season with salt and pepper to taste. Simmer over low heat for 15 to 20 minutes, stirring occasionally.

Polpette

2 While the sauce simmers, make the polpette. In a large bowl, finely crumble the tofu with your hands or with a fork. Add the parmesan, beaten eggs, onion, garlic, breadcrumbs, tamari sauce, olive oil, parsley, oregano and basil. Add salt and pepper to taste and stir until the mixture is well blended. With your hands, make 16 balls from the mixture.

3 In a deep skillet over medium heat, heat the oil and cook the polpette on each side until nicely browned and crispy. Transfer to a paper towel to absorb the excess oil.

4 Add the polpette to the tomato sauce and simmer for 5 to 10 minutes so they soak up the flavor.

5 Serve right away.

Walking Tofu Tacos

PREPARATION	COOKING	SERVINGS
15 min	10 min	4

I came across this recipe when I was scrolling online and started drooling in front of my screen. Walking tacos come from American street food: you eat them directly from a single serving chip bag. It ticks all the boxes for me, and I had to make a vegetarian version so I could enjoy it, too. It will be the hit of your next party, guaranteed!

INGREDIENTS
2 tbsp (30 mL) olive oil
1 yellow onion, chopped
1 recipe Mexican-Style Ground Tofu (page 46)
1 can (19 oz/540 mL) can cooked black beans, drained and rinsed
1 cup (133 g) corn kernels (fresh, frozen or canned)
2 tbsp (16 g) taco seasoning mix
Salt and pepper
4 small individual bags of nacho-flavored chips

Toppings
1 cup (72 g) finely chopped iceberg lettuce
2 tomatoes, seeded and diced
$\frac{1}{2}$ cup (55 g) grated cheddar cheese
$\frac{1}{4}$ cup (60 mL) Soft Tofu Sour Cream (page 36) or your choice of sour cream
$\frac{1}{4}$ cup (56 g) store-bought salsa
$\frac{1}{4}$ cup (12 g) chopped fresh cilantro

DIRECTIONS
1 In a large skillet over medium heat, heat the oil and cook the onion for 2 minutes. Add the tofu, black beans and corn, and stir. When the mixture is hot, season with taco spices and salt and pepper to taste. Simmer for 5 minutes to allow flavors to develop.

2 Gently open the tops of the chip bags.

3 Divide the tofu mixture into the chip bags. Garnish with lettuce, tomatoes, cheese, sour cream, salsa and cilantro.

4 Serve right away. Eat the walking tacos using a spoon, directly from the chip bags.

Mexican-Style
Ground Tofu

p. 46

Soft Tofu
Sour Cream

p. 36

Gourmet Salads

Barbecued Tofu Salad

PREPARATION	SERVINGS	KEEPS FOR
15 min	4	2 days in the fridge

INGREDIENTS

8 cups (280 g) mixed salad greens
  (romaine, spinach, mesclun, etc.)
1 cup (133 g) corn kernels
1 cup (150 g) cherry tomatoes,
  halved
1 avocado, diced
1 red onion, cut in strips
1 recipe Barbecued Tofu (page 50)
½ cup (125 mL) Soft Tofu Ranch
  Dressing (page 37)
Juice of 1 lime
Salt and pepper

DIRECTIONS

1 Place the mixed greens in a large salad bowl. Add the corn, cherry tomatoes, avocado and onion.

2 Coarsely chop the barbecued tofu and add it to the salad.

3 Pour the ranch dressing and lime juice over the salad. Season with salt and pepper to taste, and mix well.

4 Eat right away!

Barbecued
Tofu

p. 50

Soft Tofu
Ranch Dressing

p. 37

Mason Jar Teriyaki Tofu Salad with Tahini Dressing

PREPARATION	COOKING	SERVINGS	KEEPS FOR
20 min	25 min	4	5 days in the fridge

INGREDIENTS

Teriyaki tofu salad

1 cup (180 g) brown rice
1 cup (140 g) diced peeled butternut squash
1 cup (125 g) diced zucchini
Salt and pepper
2 tbsp (30 mL) vegetable oil
1 recipe Teriyaki Tofu (page 48)
2 cups (180 g) chopped red cabbage
2 cups (60 g) packed fresh spinach
½ cup (75 g) roasted peanuts, coarsely chopped

Tahini dressing

½ cup (120 g) tahini
Juice of 3 limes
3 tbsp (39 g) freshly grated gingerroot
3 tbsp (45 mL) pure maple syrup
2 tbsp (8 g) nutritional yeast
3 tbsp (45 mL) water
2 tbsp (30 mL) tamari sauce or soy sauce

DIRECTIONS

Teriyaki tofu salad

1 Cook the rice according to the package directions. Set aside.

2 Preheat the oven to 400°F (200°C). Line a baking sheet with parchment paper.

3 In a bowl, combine the diced squash and zucchini. Season with salt and pepper to taste. Drizzle with oil and stir. Transfer the mixture to the prepared baking sheet. Bake for 25 minutes, stirring halfway through.

Tahini dressing

4 Meanwhile, in a bowl, combine all the ingredients for the tahini dressing and mix well. Divide the dressing between four half-gallon (1.9 L) wide-mouth mason jars.

Assembly

5 Add the salad ingredients in equal portions, in layers, in each mason jar: start with the cooked rice, followed by the squash and zucchini, teriyaki tofu, cabbage, spinach and, finally, peanuts. Close the jars.

6 To serve, gently shake the jar so the dressing coats all the salad ingredients. Eat directly from the jar or transfer to a large plate or bowl.

Photo on page 130.

Teriyaki Tofu

p. 48

Mason Jar Balsamic Tofu and Strawberry Salad

PREPARATION	SERVINGS	KEEPS FOR
20 min	4	5 days in the fridge

INGREDIENTS

Dressing
¼ cup (60 mL) extra virgin olive oil
Juice of 2 lemons
2 tbsp (6 g) chopped fresh basil
Salt and pepper

Salad
1 recipe Balsamic Tofu (page 45), diced
2 cups (300 g) quartered strawberries
1 English cucumber, diced
8 cups (280 g) arugula
⅓ cup (50 g) toasted pumpkin seeds
Salt and pepper

DIRECTIONS

Dressing
1 In a bowl, combine the olive oil, lemon juice and basil. Season with salt and pepper. Divide the dressing between four half-gallon (1.9 L) wide-mouth mason jars.

Salad
2 Add the salad ingredients in equal portions, in layers, in each mason jar: start with the balsamic tofu, followed by the strawberries, cucumber, arugula and, finally, pumpkin seeds. Season with salt and pepper to taste, and close the jars.

3 To serve, gently shake the mason jar so the dressing coats all the salad ingredients. Eat directly from the jar or transfer the salad to a large plate or bowl.

Photo on page 131.

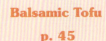

Balsamic Tofu

p. 45

Broccoli and Marinated Shallot Salad

PREPARATION	COOKING	RESTING TIME	SERVINGS	KEEPS FOR
15 min	10 min	30 min	about 4	3 days in the fridge

INGREDIENTS

4 cups (360 g) small broccoli florets
1 shallot, cut in strips
3 tbsp (45 mL) apple cider vinegar
½ cup (43 g) slivered almonds
½ recipe Tofu Feta (page 55) or
   8 oz/250 g feta of your choice,
   crumbled

Dressing

Zest and juice of 1 lemon
2 tbsp (30 mL) olive oil
2 tbsp (30 mL) pure maple syrup
Salt and pepper

DIRECTIONS

1 Fill a large bowl with ice cubes and cold water. Set aside.

2 In a large saucepan filled with boiling water, blanch the broccoli for 2 minutes. Drain quickly and plunge the broccoli into the bowl filled with ice cubes and cold water to stop the cooking. Set aside.

3 In another bowl, combine the shallot strips and vinegar. Stir and set aside.

4 In a skillet over medium heat, dry roast the slivered almonds, stirring often, for 5 to 7 minutes or until nicely browned. Remove from the heat and set aside.

5 In a salad bowl, make the dressing by mixing together the lemon zest and juice, olive oil and maple syrup. Season with salt and pepper to taste.

6 Drain the broccoli and shallot strips and place them in the salad bowl. Add the toasted almonds and stir gently to coat the ingredients with dressing. Add the tofu feta and mix gently.

7 Refrigerate the salad for at least 30 minutes before serving to allow the flavors to develop.

Tofu Feta

p. 55

Warm Bibimbap-Style Salad

PREPARATION	COOKING	SERVINGS	KEEPS FOR
30 min	20 min	about 4	3 days in the fridge

A bibimbap is a traditional Korean dish made up of a bowl of rice topped with various ingredients: vegetables, meat (usually beef), egg and hot sauce. The word "bibimbap" literally means "rice mixture." That gave me the idea of making it into a main-dish salad that is completely vegetarian thanks to tofu. It's nutritious, spicy and overflowing with umami!

INGREDIENTS

Sauce
- 1 garlic clove, chopped
- 2 tbsp (26 g) freshly grated gingerroot
- 1 tbsp tamari sauce or soy sauce
- 2 tbsp (30 mL) pure maple syrup
- 2 tsp hot pepper flakes or gochujang*
- 1 tsp seasoned rice vinegar
- 2 tsp toasted sesame oil
- 1 tbsp vegan Worcestershire sauce

Salad
- 1½ cups (270 g) brown basmati rice
- ¼ cup (60 mL) vegetable oil, divided
- 1 lb (454 g) extra-firm tofu, grated
- Salt and pepper
- 1 English cucumber, seeded and cut in four sections, then julienned
- ¼ cup (40 g) kimchi*
- 1 cup (160 g) shelled edamame
- 8 radishes, cut in rounds
- 2 cups (60 g) packed spinach, chopped
- 4 eggs**

DIRECTIONS

Sauce
1 In a bowl, combine all the sauce ingredients. Set aside.

Salad
2 Cook the rice according to the package directions. Set aside.

3 In a skillet over medium-high heat, heat 2 tbsp vegetable oil. Add the grated tofu and cook, stirring regularly, for 5 to 10 minutes or until nicely browned. Season with salt and pepper to taste. Add the sauce and cook for 2 minutes, stirring constantly. Remove from the heat and set aside.

4 In a large salad bowl, combine the rice, tofu with sauce, cucumber, kimchi, edamame, radishes and spinach. Set aside.

Toppings

2 tbsp (18 g) sesame seeds
4 green onions, chopped
Hot sauce

5 In a skillet over medium-high heat, add the rest of the oil and fry the eggs until the whites are set and the edges nicely browned.

6 Divide the salad among 4 bowls and place a fried egg on each portion. Garnish with sesame seeds, green onion and hot sauce, to taste, and serve right away.

Photo on pages 136–37.

* A key ingredient of Korean cuisine, kimchi is a fermented condiment that is increasingly popular. You can find it easily at the supermarket, in the refrigerated section of the fruits and vegetables department. Gochujang, a thick and spicy Korean sauce, can sometimes be harder to find, but if you get your hands on it, it will bring a whole other flavor dimension to this recipe!

** Omit the eggs to make the recipe vegan.

Mediterranean Salad

PREPARATION	COOKING	SERVINGS	KEEPS FOR
15 min	30 min	4	3 days in the fridge

INGREDIENTS

Dressing
3 tbsp (45 mL) olive oil
2 tbsp (30 mL) balsamic vinegar
1 tbsp Dijon mustard
1 garlic clove, chopped
Salt and pepper

Salad
$\frac{1}{2}$ cup (90 g) brown rice
$\frac{1}{2}$ cup (90 g) quinoa
1 tbsp olive oil
7 oz (200 g) halloumi cheese,*
  cubed
2 recipes Mediterranean Tofu
  (page 51), coarsely chopped
2 Lebanese cucumbers or 1 English
  cucumber, diced
$\frac{1}{2}$ cup (70 g) pitted and sliced
  olives
1 cup (180 g) diced tomatoes
$\frac{1}{2}$ red onion, sliced finely
Salt and pepper

DIRECTIONS

Dressing
1 In a bowl, combine the olive oil, balsamic vinegar, Dijon mustard and garlic and mix well. Season with salt and pepper to taste. Set aside.

Salad
2 Cook the rice and the quinoa according to the package directions. Set aside.

3 In a skillet over medium-high heat, heat the oil. Add the cubes of halloumi cheese and cook for 6 minutes, turning them halfway through, until browned. Remove from the heat and set aside.

4 In a large salad bowl, combine the rice, quinoa, halloumi cheese, Mediterranean tofu, cucumber, olives, tomatoes and onion. Pour the dressing over the salad, season with salt and pepper to taste and mix well so all the ingredients are coated in the dressing.

5 Serve right away.

* Omit the cheese to make the recipe vegan.

**Mediterranean
Tofu
p. 51**

Asian Influences

Salmon-Style Tofu Chirashi with Yum Yum Sauce

PREPARATION	SERVINGS	KEEPS FOR
40 min	4	3 days in the fridge

Chirashi is a traditional Japanese dish similar to a sushi bowl. I've been a sushi fan for years, and I thought it would be a good idea to make an appetizing vegan version featuring my delicious Salmon-Style Tofu (page 60). My Yum Yum Sauce (page 40) adds a perfect touch of umami.

INGREDIENTS

1 cup (180 g) Calrose rice
1½ tbsp seasoned rice vinegar
2 recipes Salmon-Style Tofu
   (page 60), cut in large cubes
1 English cucumber, cut in rounds
2 avocados, sliced
1 cup (150 g) grated carrots
½ cup (60 g) thinly sliced radishes
¼ cup (60 mL) Yum Yum Sauce
   (page 40)
1 nori leaf, cut in thin strips
Sesame seeds

DIRECTIONS

1 Cook the rice according to the package directions. Set aside.

2 In a large bowl, combine the rice and rice vinegar and mix well. Divide the rice among 4 small serving bowls.

3 Into each bowl, add, in equal portions, salmon-style tofu, cucumber, avocado, carrots and radishes. Garnish each bowl with 1 tbsp yum yum sauce, strips of nori and sesame seeds.

4 Serve right away.

Salmon-Style
Tofu

p. 60

Yum Yum
Sauce

p. 40

Five-Spice Tofu Buddha Bowl

PREPARATION	SERVINGS	KEEPS FOR
25 min	4	best fresh / 3 days in the fridge

INGREDIENTS

1 English cucumber
¼ cup (60 mL) seasoned rice vinegar
14 oz (400 g) rice vermicelli
2 recipes Chinese Five-Spice Tofu (page 49)
1 cup (150 g) grated carrots
1 cup (160 g) shelled edamame
1 cup (90 g) thinly sliced red cabbage
¼ cup (40 g) coarsely chopped roasted peanuts
4 green onions, minced

DIRECTIONS

1 Using a peeler or mandolin, cut the cucumber into long strips and place them in a bowl. Add the rice vinegar and set aside to marinate.

2 Cook the rice vermicelli according to the package directions. Drain and rinse with cold water. Divide the rice vermicelli among 4 small serving bowls.

3 Drain the cucumber. Into each bowl of vermicelli add, in equal portions, the five-spice tofu, drained cucumber, carrots, edamame, red cabbage, peanuts and green onions.

4 Serve right away.

Chinese
Five-Spice
Tofu

p. 49

Tofu Ramen

PREPARATION	COOKING	RESTING TIME	SERVINGS	KEEPS FOR
15 min	30 min	5 min	4	best fresh / 1 to 2 days in the fridge

INGREDIENTS

3 tbsp (45 mL) toasted sesame oil, divided
4 garlic cloves, minced
2 tbsp (26 g) freshly grated gingerroot
1 cup (125 g) julienned carrots
8 cups (2 L) vegetable broth
¼ cup (60 mL) tamari sauce or soy sauce
2 tbsp (34 g) miso paste
2 tbsp (30 mL) seasoned rice vinegar
1 tbsp pure maple syrup
2 pkg (each 10 oz/300 g) steamed ramen noodles (unflavored)
2 eggs* (in the shell)
1 lb (454 g) medium-firm tofu, cubed
4 green onions, minced
Sesame seeds
1 nori sheet, cut into thin strips
Hot sauce (optional)

DIRECTIONS

1 In a large saucepan over medium heat, heat 1 tbsp toasted sesame oil. Add the garlic, ginger and carrots. Sauté for 5 minutes or until the carrots start to soften.

2 Add the vegetable broth, tamari sauce, miso paste, rice vinegar and maple syrup. Bring to a boil over high heat. Reduce the heat to medium-low and simmer for 10 minutes to allow the flavors to develop.

3 Meanwhile, cook the ramen noodles according to the package directions. Drain and set aside.

4 Gently place the eggs in a small saucepan filled with water and bring to a boil. Remove from the heat and let the eggs sit in the hot water in the saucepan for 8 to 10 minutes. Place the eggs in a bowl of ice water for 5 minutes, then shell them and cut them in half.

5 In a skillet over medium-high heat, add the remaining toasted sesame oil and sauté the tofu cubes for 5 to 10 minutes or until nicely browned.

6 Divide the noodles equally among 4 small serving bowls. Pour the broth mixture over the top. Top each bowl with tofu, half a hard-boiled egg, green onions, sesame seeds and nori strips. Add hot sauce, if desired.

7 Serve hot.

* Omit the eggs to make the recipe vegan.

Spicy Korean Tofu Soup (Sundubu Jjigae)

PREPARATION	COOKING	SERVINGS	KEEPS FOR
15 min	25 to 30 min	4	best fresh / 1 day in the fridge

Sundubu jjigae is a delicious spicy Korean soup made with soft tofu. It can also be considered a stew, given its thick texture. Traditionally, it is served boiling hot in a terra-cotta pot and accompanied by a bowl of rice. Some people like to add a raw egg to the hot soup; it cooks gently in the soup.

INGREDIENTS

1 tbsp vegetable oil
½ onion, chopped
2 garlic cloves, minced
1 tbsp miso paste
2 tbsp (30 mL) tamari sauce or soy sauce
1 tsp smoked paprika*
2 tsp hot pepper flakes*
1 tsp cayenne pepper*
4 cups (1 L) vegetable broth
7 oz (200 g) shiitake mushrooms, stems removed, caps sliced
1 small zucchini, diced
1 carrot, diced
6 oz (175 g) smoked tofu, cut in strips
1 lb 4 oz (600 g) soft tofu
Salt and black pepper
4 green onions, minced
Sesame seeds
Hot sauce

DIRECTIONS

1 In a large saucepan over medium heat, heat the oil and sauté the onion and garlic for 3 minutes or until transparent.

2 Add the miso paste, tamari sauce, smoked paprika, hot pepper flakes and cayenne pepper, and stir. Cook for 1 minute to allow the spices to release their flavors.

3 Add the vegetable broth and bring to a boil over high heat. Reduce the heat to medium-low and add the mushrooms, zucchini, carrot and smoked tofu. Simmer for 10 minutes or until vegetables are tender.

4 Gently add the soft tofu, breaking it up into chunks as you stir. Season with salt and black pepper to taste, and simmer for 5 minutes.

5 Garnish each portion with green onion, sesame seeds and hot sauce. Serve hot.

* Traditionally, sundubu jjigae is seasoned with gochugaru. If you have this Korean spice powder at hand, use 1 tbsp (step 2) and omit the smoked paprika, hot pepper flakes and cayenne pepper.

Wonton Soup

PREPARATION	COOKING	SERVINGS	KEEPS FOR
30 min	15 min	about 4	2 to 3 days in the fridge / freeze wontons and broth separately

INGREDIENTS

Tofu wontons

8 oz (225 g) extra-firm tofu, well drained and pressed, finely crumbled
2 tbsp (30 mL) tamari sauce or soy sauce
1 tbsp toasted sesame oil
1 tbsp freshly grated gingerroot
1 garlic clove, finely chopped
Salt and pepper
1 lb (454 g) wonton wrappers, fresh or frozen and thawed

Broth

8 cups (2 L) vegetable broth
2 tbsp (30 mL) tamari sauce or soy sauce
1 tbsp seasoned rice vinegar
2 garlic cloves, finely chopped
2 tbsp (26 g) freshly grated gingerroot
1 tbsp toasted sesame oil
4 green onions, minced
2 napa cabbage leaves, cut in thin strips
Salt and pepper

DIRECTIONS

Tofu wontons

1 In a bowl, make the filling by combining the tofu, tamari sauce, sesame oil, ginger and garlic and mix well. Season with salt and pepper to taste.

2 Place a wonton wrapper on a clean work surface. Using a brush or your fingers, lightly moisten the edges of the wrapper with water.

3 Place 1 tsp of filling in the middle of the wonton wrapper. Fold the wrapper in half to form a triangle. Seal the edges well by pressing them with your fingers.

4 Repeat steps 2 and 3 with the remaining wonton wrappers and remaining filling.

Broth

5 In a large saucepan over high heat, bring the broth to a boil. Add the tamari sauce, rice vinegar, garlic, ginger, toasted sesame oil, green onions and napa cabbage. Season with salt and pepper to taste. Cover, reduce the heat to medium-low and simmer for 10 minutes.

6 While the broth simmers, bring a large saucepan of salted water to a boil. Cook the tofu wontons in the boiling water for 3 to 4 minutes or until they rise to the surface. Drain well.

Assembly

7 Add the cooked wontons to the broth and reheat for 2 minutes. Eat right away!

Japanese Curry with Tofu Katsu

PREPARATION	COOKING	SERVINGS	KEEPS FOR
30 min	40 min	4	5 days in the fridge / the curry and the tofu should be frozen separately

INGREDIENTS
Curry
- 1½ cups (270 g) long-grain white rice
- 2 tbsp (16 g) Japanese curry powder or regular curry powder
- 1 tbsp tamari sauce or soy sauce
- 1 tsp seasoned rice vinegar
- 1 tbsp pure maple syrup
- 2 tbsp (30 mL) vegetable oil
- 1 yellow onion, chopped
- 3 garlic cloves, chopped
- 2 cups (300 g) diced potatoes
- 2 cups (256 g) diced carrots
- 3 cups (750 mL) vegetable broth
- 1 tbsp water
- 1 tbsp cornstarch
- Salt and pepper

DIRECTIONS
Curry
1 Cook the rice according to the package directions. Keep warm.

2 In a small bowl, combine the curry powder, tamari sauce, rice vinegar and maple syrup.

3 In a large saucepan over medium heat, heat the oil and cook the onion for 2 minutes. Add the garlic and cook for 1 minute. Add the potatoes, carrots, reserved spice mixture and broth. Bring to a boil over high heat. Reduce the heat to low, cover and simmer for 15 minutes.

4 In a small bowl, combine the water and cornstarch. Add the mixture to the saucepan, stir and cook uncovered for 5 to 7 minutes. Season with salt and pepper to taste. Remove from the heat and keep warm.

Tofu katsu

6 cups (1.5 L) canola oil (for frying)
2 blocks (each 1 lb/454 g) extra-firm
   tofu
2 beaten eggs
$\frac{1}{2}$ cup (68 g) all-purpose flour
$\frac{1}{2}$ cup (30 g) nutritional yeast,
   divided
2 tsp smoked paprika, divided
2 tsp garlic powder, divided
Salt and pepper
$\frac{3}{4}$ cup (45 g) panko breadcrumbs
3 green onions, chopped

Tofu katsu

5 In a deep fryer or a large, deep saucepan, heat the oil to 350°F (180°C).

6 Meanwhile, cut the tofu blocks in half lengthwise to mimic the size and thickness of a chicken breast. If desired, cut the pieces into the shape of chicken breasts.

7 Pour the beaten eggs into a bowl.

8 In a second bowl, combine the flour, half the nutritional yeast, half the smoked paprika, half the garlic powder, and salt and pepper to taste.

9 In a third bowl, combine the panko breadcrumbs, the remaining nutritional yeast, the remaining smoked paprika and the remaining garlic powder. Season with salt and pepper to taste.

10 Coat each piece of tofu well, first with the beaten eggs, then the flour mixture and finally the panko breadcrumbs mixture.

11 Fry the tofu pieces in the hot oil for 6 minutes, turning them halfway through. Transfer to a paper towel to remove any excess oil, then sprinkle with salt.

Assembly

12 In a large serving bowl, add the rice and cover with the curry. Garnish with crispy tofu pieces and green onions and serve right away.

Photo on pages 154–155.

Teriyaki Tofu Spring Rolls

PREPARATION	MAKES	KEEPS FOR
30 min	8 rolls	best fresh / 2 days in the fridge in plastic wrap

INGREDIENTS

16 rice paper wrappers
16 leaves Boston lettuce
1 recipe Teriyaki Tofu (page 48), cut
   in strips
1 English cucumber, seeded and
   julienned
1 cup (150 g) grated carrots
1 avocado, cut in thin slices
Fresh mint leaves
Fresh cilantro leaves
1 recipe Yum Yum Sauce (page 40)

DIRECTIONS

1 Fill a large bowl with warm water. Soak 2 rice wrappers in the water for a few seconds to moisten them. Stick one on top of the other and place them on a clean work surface.

2 In the middle of the double rice wrap, place horizontally 2 lettuce leaves, teriyaki tofu strips, cucumber, carrots, avocado and a few mint leaves and cilantro leaves.

3 Fold the sides of the double rice wrap over the filling, then fold the bottom over the top and roll the whole wrap tightly. Repeat the process for the other spring rolls.

4 Serve right away with yum yum sauce.

Teriyaki Tofu
p. 48
Yum Yum Sauce
p. 40

Butter Tofu

PREPARATION	COOKING	SERVINGS	KEEPS FOR
15 min	20 min	4	5 days in the fridge / can be frozen

INGREDIENTS

¼ cup (60 g) ghee* or clarified butter (or plant-based butter), divided
1 lb (454 g) extra-firm tofu, broken into pieces with your hands
1 onion, finely chopped
1 garlic clove, finely chopped
1 tbsp freshly grated gingerroot
1½ tbsp ground cumin
1 tbsp chili powder
½ tsp garam masala
1½ tbsp ground coriander
Salt and pepper
1½ cups (375 mL) tomato sauce
1 cup (250 mL) 15% cooking cream or heavy or whipping (35%) cream**
1 tsp pure maple syrup
Fresh cilantro leaves

Sides

Cooked basmati rice
Naan bread

DIRECTIONS

1 In a large skillet over medium-high heat, heat half the ghee and brown the tofu pieces on all sides until crispy. Transfer the tofu to a plate. Reduce the heat to medium, add the remaining ghee and sauté the onion until transparent. Add the garlic and ginger and sauté for 1 minute or until they release their aroma.

2 Add the cumin, chili powder, garam masala and coriander. Season with salt and pepper to taste, and stir to coat the tofu.

3 Add the tomato sauce and cream to the pan. Stir until the sauce is well blended. Simmer for a few minutes, until the sauce thickens slightly.

4 Add the maple syrup and season with salt and pepper to taste.

5 Add the tofu cubes to the sauce and stir. Simmer over low heat for 5 minutes or until the tofu is cooked through.

6 Garnish with fresh cilantro and serve right away with basmati rice and/or naan bread.

* Ghee is a type of clarified butter mainly used in Indian and other South Asian cuisine. It is sold in many supermarkets but can be replaced by butter or clarified butter you make yourself.
** Use a plant-based cream to make the recipe vegan.

Shredded Korean Tofu Soft Tacos

PREPARATION	COOKING	MAKES	KEEPS FOR
20 min	15 min	8 tacos	2 to 3 days in the fridge

INGREDIENTS

Shredded Korean tofu

1 lb (454 g) extra-firm tofu
⅓ cup (75 mL) tamari sauce or soy sauce
⅓ cup (75 mL) pure maple syrup
¼ cup (60 g) ketchup
3 tbsp (45 mL) seasoned rice vinegar
1 tbsp hot pepper flakes
1½ tbsp toasted sesame oil
1 tbsp vegetable oil
2 garlic cloves, minced
1 tsp freshly grated gingerroot
Salt and black pepper
1 tbsp sesame seeds
2 green onions, chopped

Tacos

8 soft corn or flour tortillas
2 cups (180 g) shredded napa cabbage
2 Lebanese cucumbers or 1 English cucumber, cut in thin rounds
1 cup (150 g) grated carrots
½ cup (75 g) kimchi
Hot sauce (optional)

DIRECTIONS

Shredded Korean tofu

1 Drain the tofu and blot it in a clean towel. Grate the tofu and set aside.

2 In a bowl, combine the tamari sauce, maple syrup, ketchup, rice vinegar and hot pepper flakes. Set aside.

3 In a skillet over medium heat, heat the sesame oil and vegetable oil. Add the garlic and ginger, and sauté for 1 to 2 minutes or until they release their aroma.

4 Increase the heat to medium-high and add the grated tofu. Season with salt and black pepper to taste, and sauté for 5 to 7 minutes or until the tofu is browned.

5 Pour the sauce into the pan and stir to coat the tofu well. Cook for 2 to 3 minutes to allow the flavors to develop.

6 Remove from the heat and sprinkle with sesame seeds and chopped green onions.

Tacos

7 Heat the tortillas according to the package directions.

8 Garnish each tortilla with one portion of shredded Korean tofu, cabbage, cucumber, carrots, kimchi and hot sauce, if desired.

9 Serve right away.

Cajun Tofu Sushirritos

PREPARATION	RESTING TIME	MAKES	KEEPS FOR
1 hour	15 to 20 min	4	best fresh / 2 days in the fridge

Sushirritos are a fusion dish whose name is a combination of "sushi" and "burrito." Rolled in nori sheets like maki, they are then cut in half. You eat them a bit like a burrito. They are great for lunch or for eating on the run! I've always liked non-traditional sushi, and this one in particular: it features my Cajun Tofu (page 44) and flavors that move away completely from Japanese cuisine. The result is absolutely incredible! Try them – they're addictive!

INGREDIENTS

Herb yogurt sauce
½ cup (125 g) plain Greek yogurt*
¼ cup (15 g) packed fresh parsley leaves
3 tbsp (9 g) fresh dill
1 tbsp fresh chives
1 garlic clove
1 tbsp fresh lemon juice
1 tbsp apple cider vinegar
Salt and pepper

Rice
1 cup (180 g) Calrose rice
2 tbsp (30 mL) seasoned rice vinegar

DIRECTIONS

Herb yogurt sauce
1 In a blender, on high speed, combine the yogurt, parsley, dill, chives, garlic, lemon juice and vinegar until smooth. Season with salt and pepper to taste. Set aside in the fridge.

Rice
2 Cook the rice according to the package directions.

3 Add the rice vinegar to the hot rice. Stir gently to distribute the vinegar evenly. Let cool for 15 to 20 minutes.

* Use plant-based yogurt to make the recipe vegan.

Sushirritos

4 nori sheets
1 recipe Cajun Tofu (page 44)
2 cups (180 g) thinly sliced red
  cabbage
1 English cucumber, seeded and
  julienned
1 avocado, sliced finely
Hot sauce (optional)

Sushirritos

4 Pour 2 cups (500 mL) warm water into a bowl. Let cool for 15 to 20 minutes.

5 On a clean, dry work surface or on a bamboo mat covered with plastic wrap, place a nori sheet, rough side up.

6 Moisten your hands with water so the rice doesn't stick. Take some rice (about the size of a tennis ball) and spread it out in an even layer on the nori sheet, leaving a $\frac{3}{4}$-inch (2 cm) border uncovered at the top of the sheet.

7 Place a portion of Cajun tofu in the middle of the rice, then the red cabbage, cucumber and avocado.

8 Using the bamboo mat or with your hands, roll the nori sheet over the filling, squeezing gently to make a roll. Lightly moisten the uncovered edge of the nori sheet with water to seal the sushirrito.

9 Repeat the process with the other nori sheets and the remaining ingredients.

10 Using a sharp knife, cut the sushirritos diagonally in half. Serve with the herb yogurt sauce as a dip and with hot sauce, if desired.

Photo on pages 164–165.

Cajun Tofu

p. 44

100% Comfort Food

Creamy Tofu Pasta, Kale and Butternut Squash Stew

PREPARATION	COOKING	SERVINGS	KEEPS FOR
20 min	35 min	6	5 days in the fridge / can be frozen

INGREDIENTS

3 tbsp (45 mL) olive oil
2 shallots, chopped
1 garlic clove, chopped
1 lb (454 g) extra-firm tofu,
  crumbled with your hands
2½ cups (350 g) diced peeled
  butternut squash
2 tsp smoked paprika
1 tbsp dried Italian seasoning
3 cups (750 mL) vegetable broth
2 cups (500 mL) milk or plain
  unsweetened plant-based
  beverage
6 cups (510 g) scoobi doo
  (cavatappi) pasta*
2 cups (140 g) chopped kale leaves
Salt and pepper
3 cups (336 g) grated sharp
  cheddar cheese,** divided

DIRECTIONS

1 Preheat the oven to 350°F (180°C).

2 In an oven-safe saucepan over medium heat, heat the oil and sauté the shallots, garlic, tofu, squash, smoked paprika and Italian seasoning for 8 minutes.

3 Add the broth and cook, covered, for 4 minutes.

4 Add the milk, pasta and kale. Season with salt and pepper to taste, then stir. Cook until the pasta is al dente.

5 Remove from the heat and add 1 cup (112 g) cheddar. Stir and adjust the seasonings as needed.

6 Top with the remaining cheese. Bake for 10 minutes. Set the oven to broil and brown for 1 or 2 minutes.

7 Serve right away.

* You can replace the scoobi doo pasta, a popular variety in some parts of the U.S. and Canada, with any other short pasta.

** Use grated dairy-free cheddar-style cheese to make the recipe vegan.

Lasagna with Tofu Tomato Sauce

PREPARATION	COOKING	RESTING TIME	SERVINGS	KEEPS FOR
30 min	40 to 45 min	5 to 10 min	6 to 8	5 days in the fridge / can be frozen

INGREDIENTS

Tofu tomato sauce

2 tbsp (30 mL) olive oil

1 onion, chopped

2 garlic cloves, chopped

1 recipe Spicy Sausage Meat–Style Tofu (page 59)

1 can (28 oz/796 mL) crushed tomatoes

2 tbsp (34 g) tomato paste

1 tsp dried oregano

1 tsp dried basil

Salt and pepper

DIRECTIONS

Tofu tomato sauce

1 In a large saucepan over medium heat, heat the oil and sauté the onion for 3 minutes or until transparent. Add the garlic and cook for 2 minutes or until it releases its aroma. Add the spicy sausage meat–style tofu and cook, stirring often, for 3 to 5 minutes or until lightly browned.

2 Add the tomatoes, tomato paste, oregano and basil and mix well. Season with salt and pepper to taste. Reduce the heat to medium-low and simmer the sauce uncovered, stirring occasionally, for 5 to 10 minutes or until it thickens slightly. Set aside.

Spicy Sausage Meat–Style Tofu

p. 59

Lasagna

12 lasagna noodles
2 cups (500 g) ricotta
Salt and pepper
2 cups (224 g) grated mozzarella
cheese
½ cup (25 g) grated parmesan
cheese

Lasagna

3 Preheat the oven to 350°F (180°C). Grease a 13 x 9-inch (33 x 23 cm) baking dish.

4 Cook the lasagna noodles according to the package directions. Drain.

5 In a bowl, combine the ricotta with a pinch of salt and pepper and mix well.

6 In the prepared dish, spread a thin layer of tomato sauce. Add a first layer of cooked lasagna noodles. Spread some of the ricotta mixture over the lasagna noodles, then some of the sauce. Sprinkle with half the mozzarella and half the grated parmesan.

7 Continue the process with the rest of the noodles, ricotta mixture and sauce. Add the rest of the mozzarella and parmesan on top.

8 Cover the baking dish with aluminum foil and bake for 25 to 30 minutes. Remove the aluminum foil and continue cooking for 10 to 15 minutes or until the top of the lasagna is browned and it is hot and bubbling.

9 Let rest for a few minutes before serving.

Photo on pages 172–173.

Vol-au-Vent-Style Casserole

PREPARATION	COOKING	SERVINGS	KEEPS FOR
20 min	30 min	4	5 days in the fridge / can be frozen

Nothing makes me happier than eating a steaming casserole when the temperature drops below zero. I wanted to share with you my version of comfort food par excellence: vol-au-vent casserole! It's a dish I loved especially when I was a little girl, so I wanted to create a vegetarian version that was just as delicious.

INGREDIENTS

2 tbsp (30 g) butter,* divided
1 lb (454 g) extra-firm tofu, broken
    into small pieces with your fingers
Salt and pepper
1 tbsp vegetable oil
1 loaf ciabatta bread, cubed
½ yellow onion, chopped
1 carrot, diced
1½ tsp herbes de Provence
1 tbsp all-purpose flour
1 cup (250 mL) milk*
½ cup (125 mL) vegetable broth
½ cup (67 g) corn kernels
½ cup (67 g) green peas
1½ cups (168 g) grated cheddar
    cheese*

DIRECTIONS

1 Preheat the oven to 375°F (190°C).

2 In a skillet over medium-high heat, heat half the butter. Add the tofu pieces and salt and pepper to taste. Sauté for 5 to 10 minutes or until the tofu is browned. Remove the tofu pieces from the pan and set aside.

3 In the same pan, over medium-high heat, heat the vegetable oil and cook the bread cubes for 5 minutes or until crispy. Remove from the pan and set aside.

4 In the same pan, over medium heat, add the remaining butter and sauté the onion, carrot and herbes de Provence for 3 to 4 minutes.

5 Add the flour. Add the milk and vegetable broth and bring to a boil, stirring often, over medium-high heat. When the sauce thickens, add the corn, peas and tofu. Season with salt and pepper to taste, and stir.

6 Transfer the mixture to a baking dish. Garnish with croutons and grated cheese. Bake for 5 minutes. Broil and brown for 2 to 3 minutes.

7 Let rest for 5 minutes before serving.

* Use plant-based butter, dairy-free milk and grated dairy-free cheddar-style cheese to make the recipe vegan.

Balsamic Tofu Caprese

PREPARATION	COOKING	SERVINGS	KEEPS FOR
5 min	10 min	6	3 days in the fridge

INGREDIENTS

2 recipes Balsamic Tofu (page 45)
12 oz (375 g) fresh mozzarella cheese balls, sliced
2 cups (300 g) cherry tomatoes, halved
1 tbsp olive oil
Salt and pepper
$\frac{1}{2}$ cup (15 g) packed fresh basil leaves, chopped
Store-bought balsamic glaze

Suggested sides

Pasta with sauce
Salad
Toast

DIRECTIONS

1 Preheat the oven to 450°F (230°C).

2 Arrange the tofu pieces in a baking dish. On each piece, place slices of mozzarella. Add the cherry tomatoes and olive oil. Season with salt and pepper to taste.

3 Bake for 7 to 8 minutes, set the oven to broil and broil for 1 to 2 minutes.

4 Garnish with chopped basil and a drizzle of balsamic glaze. Serve right away, along with pasta with sauce, a salad or toast, if desired.

Balsamic Tofu
p. 45

Cajun Tofu Rigatoni

PREPARATION	COOKING	SERVINGS	KEEPS FOR
10 min	15 min	4	5 days in the fridge / can be frozen

INGREDIENTS
1 lb (454 g) rigatoni
2 tbsp (30 g) butter*
½ yellow onion, finely chopped
2 garlic cloves, chopped
2 tomatoes, grated**
1 cup (133 g) corn kernels
2 tsp Cajun spices
1½ cups (375 mL) 15% cooking
   cream or heavy or whipping
   (35%) cream*
½ cup (25 g) grated parmesan
   cheese*
Salt and pepper
1 recipe Cajun Tofu (page 44)
¼ cup (15 g) chopped fresh parsley

DIRECTIONS
1 Cook the rigatoni according to the package directions. Drain, keeping ¼ cup (60 mL) of the cooking water. Set aside.

2 In a large skillet over medium heat, heat the butter and sauté the onion for 2 minutes or until transparent.

3 Add the garlic and sauté for 1 minute.

4 Add the tomatoes, corn and Cajun spices. Stir and cook, stirring occasionally, for 2 minutes or until the vegetables start to soften.

5 Reduce the heat to low and add the cream, parmesan, and salt and pepper to taste. Stir and simmer for 2 minutes or until sauce thickens slightly.

6 Add the cooked rigatoni, reserved cooking water and Cajun tofu. Remove from the heat. Add the parsley, season with salt and pepper to taste, and stir.

7 Divide among 4 bowls and enjoy!

* Use plant-based butter, dairy-free cooking cream and grated dairy-free parmesan-style cheese to make the recipe vegan.
** To grate tomatoes, use the shredding side of a cheese grater. This way, you will be left with only the skin in your hand, and you will quickly get a nice purée!

Cajun Tofu

p. 44

Vegetable, Rice and Soft Tofu Soup

PREPARATION	COOKING	SERVINGS	KEEPS FOR
15 min	45 min	4	3 days in the fridge / can be frozen

INGREDIENTS

1 tbsp olive oil
1 tbsp butter or plant-based butter
1 onion, chopped
2 garlic cloves, minced
2 carrots, peeled and cut in rounds
2 celery stalks, diced
2 cups (180 g) small broccoli florets
½ cup (90 g) brown rice
5 cups (1.25 L) vegetable broth
1 tsp dried thyme
1 tsp dried basil
Salt and pepper
5 oz (150 g) soft tofu
¼ cup (60 mL) unsweetened plain
   soy beverage
Juice of ½ lemon
2 tbsp (8 g) nutritional yeast
1 tbsp pure maple syrup
1 cup (133 g) corn kernels

DIRECTIONS

1 In a large saucepan over medium heat, heat the oil and butter. Sauté the onion and garlic for 2 to 3 minutes or until they are tender and release their aroma.

2 Add the carrots, celery and broccoli and sauté for 5 minutes, stirring frequently.

3 Add the brown rice and stir. Add the broth, stir and bring to a boil over high heat. Reduce the heat to medium-low and add the thyme, basil, and salt and pepper to taste. Cover and simmer for 25 minutes or until the rice and vegetables are tender.

4 Meanwhile, in a blender, combine the soft tofu, soy beverage, lemon juice, nutritional yeast and maple syrup and blend until smooth and creamy.

5 Remove the saucepan from the heat and gently add the creamy tofu mixture to the soup.

6 Return the saucepan to low heat and add the corn. Season with salt and pepper to taste. Stir the soup and reheat without letting it boil.

7 Serve piping hot.

Photo on page 183.

Tofu Noodle Soup

PREPARATION	COOKING	SERVINGS	KEEPS FOR
10 min	25 min	4	5 days in the fridge / can be frozen

I was a big fan of chicken noodle soup in the days when I ate meat. To me, it's real comfort in a bowl. I've been thinking about it for years, and I finally took the time to make a 100% vegan version that is just as comforting: tofu noodle soup!

INGREDIENTS

2 tbsp (30 mL) vegetable oil
1 lb (454 g) extra-firm tofu, broken
 into small pieces with your hands
2 tbsp (8 g) nutritional yeast
Salt and pepper
1 onion, chopped
2 garlic cloves, minced
2 carrots, cut in thin rounds
2 celery stalks, diced
8 cups (2 L) vegetable broth*
7 oz (200 g) spaghettini, broken into
 small pieces (about 1$\frac{1}{2}$ cups/
 375 mL)
2 tbsp (30 mL) tamari sauce or soy
 sauce
1 tbsp lemon juice
1 tbsp poultry seasoning mixture
1 tbsp dried parsley
$\frac{1}{2}$ tsp ground turmeric

DIRECTIONS

1 In a large saucepan over medium heat, heat the oil. Add the tofu and sprinkle it with the nutritional yeast. Season with salt and pepper to taste, and brown on all sides for 5 to 10 minutes. Remove the tofu from the saucepan and set aside.

2 In the same saucepan, add the onion, garlic, carrots and celery. Sauté for 5 minutes or until the vegetables start to soften.

3 Add the vegetable broth and bring to a boil over high heat. Reduce the heat to medium-low and simmer for 10 minutes or until the vegetables are tender.

4 Meanwhile, in a large saucepan of boiling salted water, cook the spaghettini according to the package directions. Drain and set aside.

5 Add the tofu to the soup along with the tamari sauce, lemon juice, poultry seasoning mixture, parsley and turmeric. Stir and simmer for 5 minutes to allow the flavors to develop.

6 Season with salt and pepper to taste. Add the cooked spaghettini and mix well. Serve right away.

Photo on page 182.

* You can get vegan broth concentrate that mimics chicken broth. Feel free to use it instead of vegetable broth!

Mamie Claire's Long Macaroni with Tomato Sauce

PREPARATION	COOKING	SERVINGS	KEEPS FOR
15 min	30 min	4	4 days in the fridge

This is a really simple recipe, but it's my favorite one in the book: it's from my grandmother Mamie Claire, who left us too soon. She raised six children on her own, on very little money. When my cousins and I were little, she would make us long macaroni with a tomato and ground beef sauce that we loved. Here's a vegetarian version. I hope it will be as comforting for you as it is for me.

INGREDIENTS

10 oz (300 g) long macaroni or bucatini
1 tbsp butter or vegetable oil
1 recipe Ground Beef–Style Tofu (page 58)
1 tsp ground cloves
1 tsp ground cinnamon
1 tbsp pure maple syrup
Salt and pepper
1 can (19 oz/540 mL) tomato juice
1 can (28 oz/796 mL) diced tomatoes
4 slices orange processed cheese (Velveeta or Kraft Singles type)

DIRECTIONS

1 In a large saucepan of boiling salted water, cook the macaroni according to the package directions. Drain and set aside.

2 In a large skillet over medium heat, heat the butter and sauté the ground beef–style tofu for 2 to 3 minutes. Add the cloves, cinnamon and maple syrup. Season with salt and pepper to taste, and stir. Cook for 1 to 2 minutes to allow the flavors to develop.

3 Add the tomato juice and canned tomatoes. Stir and bring to a boil. Reduce the heat to medium-low and simmer, stirring occasionally, for 10 to 15 minutes or until the sauce thickens slightly.

4 To serve, place a slice of cheese in the middle of each plate, then the macaroni. Top with the sauce and enjoy.

Ground Beef–Style Tofu
p. 58

Room for Dessert!

Chocolate Pie

PREPARATION	COOKING	RESTING TIME	MAKES	KEEPS FOR
20 min	10 min	at least 2 hours 30 min	1 pie (6 servings)	3 to 4 days in the fridge

Soft tofu is perfect for giving mixtures a smooth and creamy texture. It is an ideal dessert ingredient. Because I love pie and chocolate, I made soft tofu a key ingredient in . . . chocolate pie! You can serve it with whipped cream, fresh berries or toasted nuts.

INGREDIENTS

Chocolate crust
1 1/2 cups (192 g) chocolate cookie crumbs
6 tbsp (90 g) melted butter*

Filling
12 oz (375 g) semi-sweet chocolate, chopped (about 2 cups/500 mL)
10 oz (300 g) soft tofu, well drained
1/2 cup (60 g) confectioners' (icing) sugar
1 tsp vanilla extract
1/4 tsp salt

DIRECTIONS

Chocolate crust
1 Preheat the oven to 350°F (180°C). Grease a 9-inch (23 cm) pie plate.

2 In a bowl, combine the cookie crumbs and butter until you get a sandy consistency.

3 Press the crumb mixture into the prepared pie plate and bake for 10 minutes. Let cool.

Filling
4 In a double boiler or microwave,** melt the chocolate. Let cool slightly.

5 In a food processor, combine the soft tofu, confectioners' sugar, vanilla and salt and process until smooth and creamy. Add the melted chocolate and process until well mixed.

6 Pour the chocolate filling into the cooled crust and smooth the surface.

7 Refrigerate the pie for at least 2 hours or until set.

8 Slice and enjoy.

* Use melted plant-based butter to make the recipe vegan.
** In the microwave, to avoid a mess, heat the chocolate for 30 seconds at a time. Stir after each 30 seconds until the chocolate is completely melted and smooth.

Chai Crème Brûlée

PREPARATION	COOKING	RESTING TIME	SERVINGS	KEEPS FOR
20 min	40 min	at least 4 hours	4	2 to 3 days in the fridge (or overnight)

INGREDIENTS

¼ cup (60 mL) oat beverage
3 chai tea bags or 4 tsp chai spice mix
3 tbsp (24 g) cornstarch
3 tbsp (45 mL) water
10 oz (300 g) soft tofu, well drained
½ cup (60 g) confectioners' (icing) sugar
1 tsp vanilla extract
¼ cup (53 g) packed brown sugar

DIRECTIONS

1 Preheat the oven to 325°F (160°C).

2 In a small saucepan over medium heat, heat the oat beverage until it steams, without letting it boil. Remove from the heat and steep the chai tea bags for 5 to 7 minutes. Remove the tea bags.

3 In a small bowl, combine the cornstarch and water.

4 In a food processor, combine the tofu, confectioners' sugar, vanilla, oat beverage and cornstarch mixture and process until smooth and creamy.

5 Divide the mixture into 4 ramekins and place them in a baking dish with high sides. Fill the baking dish with hot water halfway up the ramekins.

6 Bake for 30 minutes or until the custard is firm but still slightly jiggly in the middle.

7 Remove the ramekins from the water bath and let cool for about 10 minutes. Refrigerate for at least 4 hours, preferably overnight.

8 Before serving, sprinkle each crème brûlée with 1 tbsp brown sugar. Using a kitchen blowtorch, burn the sugar until it is golden and caramelized. Eat right away.

Photo on pages 190–191.

Donut Holes

PREPARATION	COOKING	MAKES	KEEPS FOR
15 min	15 min	about 12	best fresh / 1 to 2 days at room temperature

My grandma Gigi is a real pro when it comes to desserts. One of her specialties is donuts and donut holes, which she sprinkles with confectioners' sugar. As a child, I ate tons of them when I went to her house, and I still do the same every year at Christmas. As a tribute to her, I decided to make my own version, entirely vegan and lighter, with my Soft Tofu Sour Cream (page 36). I hope you like them, Mamie!

INGREDIENTS

1 cup (120 g) cake flour or all-
    purpose flour
2 tsp baking powder
½ cup (100 g) granulated sugar
1 pinch of salt
1 cup (250 mL) Soft Tofu Sour
    Cream (page 36)
1 tsp vanilla extract
5 cups (1.25 L) canola oil (for frying)
Confectioners' (icing) sugar
    (optional)
Your choice of jam (optional)

DIRECTIONS

1 In a bowl, combine the flour, baking powder, granulated sugar and salt.

2 Add the sour cream and vanilla, and stir until smooth.

3 In a large saucepan or deep fryer, heat the oil to 350°F (180°C).

4 Using a teaspoon, scoop up some dough and gently place it in the hot oil. Fry the donut holes for 2 to 3 minutes on each side or until golden and crispy, turning them as needed so they cook evenly.

5 Remove the fried donut holes using a slotted spoon and place them on paper towels to absorb the excess oil. If desired, sprinkle with confectioners' sugar while still hot.

6 Let cool slightly before eating. You can serve them with your choice of jam for dipping.

Photo on pages 194–195.

**Soft Tofu
Sour Cream**

p. 36

Tiramisu

PREPARATION	RESTING TIME	SERVINGS	KEEPS FOR
20 min	at least 4 hours (or overnight)	4	2 to 3 days in the fridge

INGREDIENTS

1 lb (454 g) medium-firm tofu, well drained and pressed

⅔ cup (80 g) confectioners' (icing) sugar

1 tbsp vanilla extract

1 pkg (7 oz/200 g) ladyfingers* (about 24)

1 cup (250 mL) strong coffee, cooled

Unsweetened cocoa powder

DIRECTIONS

1 In a food processor, combine the tofu, confectioners' sugar and vanilla and process until smooth and creamy. Set aside.

2 Quickly dip the ladyfingers, one at a time, in the cooled coffee to soak without letting them get too soft.

3 Arrange a first layer of soaked biscuits in a serving dish. Pour half the tofu mixture over the biscuits and spread evenly.

4 Add a second layer of soaked biscuits, then spread the remaining tofu mixture on top.

5 Cover and refrigerate for at least 4 hours or overnight to allow the tiramisu to set and for the flavors to develop.

6 Before serving, sprinkle generously with cocoa powder.

* Unfortunately, ladyfingers are not vegan. Feel free to replace them with sweetened soft vegan cookies.

Lemon Raspberry Cake

PREPARATION	COOKING	SERVINGS	KEEPS FOR
About 20 min	45 to 55 min	8 to 10	5 days in the fridge

INGREDIENTS

1½ cups (202 g) all-purpose flour
2 tsp baking powder
½ tsp salt
10 oz (300 g) soft tofu
1⅓ cups (233 g) plus 2 tbsp (25 g)
    granulated sugar
3 large eggs
Zest of 2 lemons
2½ tbsp (37 mL) lemon juice
½ tsp vanilla extract
½ cup (125 mL) vegetable oil
1½ cups (195 g) fresh or frozen and
    thawed raspberries

Glaze

1 cup (120 g) confectioners' (icing)
    sugar
2 tbsp (30 mL) lemon juice

DIRECTIONS

1 Preheat the oven to 350°F (180°C). Grease a 9-inch (23 cm) cake pan or line it with parchment paper.

2 In a bowl, combine the flour, baking powder and salt. Set aside.

3 In a large bowl, with an electric mixer, beat the soft tofu until smooth. Add 1⅓ cups (233 g) granulated sugar, eggs, lemon zest, lemon juice, vanilla and oil. Beat to mix well.

4 Add the dry ingredients to the wet ingredients. Using a spatula, mix until smooth. Pour half the batter into the prepared pan.

5 In a small bowl, combine the raspberries and the remaining 2 tbsp (25 g) sugar. Spread this mixture evenly over the batter in the pan. Pour the remaining batter over the raspberries.

6 Bake for 45 to 55 minutes or until a toothpick inserted in the middle of the cake comes out clean.

7 Let the cake cool in the pan for 15 minutes, then remove from the pan and let cool on a rack.

8 In a bowl, combine the confectioners' sugar and lemon juice and mix until it forms a smooth glaze.

9 Once the cake is completely cool, drizzle the glaze on top. Let the glaze set before serving.

Oreo Cookie Iced Tofu

PREPARATION	RESTING TIME	SERVINGS	KEEPS FOR
15 min	at least 4 hours	about 4 to 6	1 to 2 weeks in the freezer

Did you know that Oreo cookies are entirely vegan? That makes them the perfect choice for a frozen dessert that is also entirely vegan and ultra smooth thanks to soft tofu. Warning: you'll get hooked!

INGREDIENTS

1 lb 4 oz (600 g) soft tofu
1 cup (120 g) confectioners' (icing) sugar
2 tsp vanilla extract
Pinch of salt
20 Oreo cookies (or more, if you like)

DIRECTIONS

1 Drain the soft tofu in a fine-mesh sieve, squeezing to remove as much liquid as possible.

2 In a food processor, combine the drained soft tofu, confectioners' sugar, vanilla and salt until smooth and creamy. Transfer to a bowl and set aside.

3 Crush the Oreo cookies using a rolling pin or place them in a sealable plastic bag and crush them with a heavy object.

4 Add the Oreo cookie crumbs to the tofu mixture and mix with a spatula to distribute the cookie pieces evenly in the mixture.

5 Pour the mixture into a sealable container, preferably metal to facilitate freezing. Spread out the mixture with a spatula.

6 Seal the container and place in the freezer for at least 4 hours or until the mixture is firm.

7 Before serving, let the iced tofu soften so it's easy to serve with an ice cream scoop.

8 Serve in bowls or cones and enjoy.

Recipe Index

Index by Tofu Texture

Index of Basic Recipes

Acknowledgments

Authors often conclude their acknowledgments with words to their readers and the people who follow them on social media. I couldn't start mine without addressing the La Fraîche gang. Without knowing it, you were my muses in creating this book. It was in seeing your appetite for tofu that I got the idea of devoting a whole book to this food you love so much, to offer you all the recipes you need to cook it in all sorts of ways. Eternal thanks for inspiring me and following me with so much interest for all these years. I hope Everything Tofu will fill you with happiness and will become an essential guide in your kitchens.

Next, I would like to thank my incredible team: the entire Éditions de l'Homme family. Thank you to Florence Bisch for being my plus-one at the 2023 DUX awards gala. Who would have thought that a passionate discussion about tofu would lead to the creation of this gem? Thanks to you, my idea could germinate in the whole team, and I can't thank you enough. Thanks to Sophie Aumais for jumping into the concept with both feet and for being this book's number-one fan even before it was written. I can't wait for you to make my recipes! Thank you to my friend and publisher Marianne Prairie, the best, who believes in me more than I believe in myself, who is always ready to listen, present and 1,000-percent invested in each of my ideas. You are amazing! Thanks to Grace Cheong and Julien Rodrigue, whom, to my great delight, I was able to bring together for a second adventure, and to Roxane Vaillant, all three of whom were responsible for the book's impeccable look. You are true magicians. I am always dazzled by your flawless work, which is so true to what I had pictured. Finally, thank you to all those who worked, from near or far, to make Everything Tofu relevant, accurate, vibrant and, above all, in three dimensions. Holding it in my hands is a dream come true, and I couldn't be more grateful.

And now for my two treasures from this project: Ariel Tarr and Chantal Legault. Professional encounters that leave their mark and change everything are so rare. From the first moment the three of us went into the studio, we knew it was the start of something special. Ariel, thank you for your eye, talent, gentleness and ability to listen, plus your coffees, your carts, your studio, your paint-covered fingers and your unfailing good humor. You understood right away the atmosphere and the imagery I was hoping to get for my photos, which make this book spectacular. Chantal, thank you for your incredible generosity, your presence, your laughter, your expertise, your creativity, your Chinese cookies, your cups of Rooibos tea, your dedication, your dishes in industrial quantities and your remarkable personality. I have rarely seen someone plate food with so much energy, passion and skill. (Special thanks to your son Thomas, our official recipe tester, who gave me positive and constructive feedback, allowing me to put the finishing touches on this book.) You are exceptional women. How lucky was I to have you by my side for four weeks! The photos are perfect.

To conclude, I would like to direct my words to the people close to me, my family and friends. You are the most precious things in my life. Thank you for being so present and for encouraging me with so much love in all that I do. My online magazine La Fraîche would not exist without you and your support. Pounet, Mounette, Dada, my love (Guillaume), Mamie, Papi, my Girlicious and better half, my park pals, Marjo, Beth, Kame, Mémé, Kim, my framboise, Caroune, Natalia for my amazing nails, JF for the fabulous face on the cover, Virginie, Béatrice, Mel and Medhi, Benzok and my wonderful and large Auger-Demarbre, Simard and Guilbault families. I am so spoiled to be so well supported.

I love you! XOXOXOXO
Merci, merci, merci!
My heart is full,

Eve-Lyne